Noel Sickles

ILLUSTRATORS

The Eleventh Annual
National Exhibition of Illustration
held in the Galleries of the
Society of Illustrators
128 East 63rd Street, New York
January 20 through February 28, 1969

THE ELEVENTH ANNUAL OF AMERICAN ILLUSTRATION

Published for the Society of Illustrators

Editor: Herb Mott

Designer: Charles A. Long

Hastings House, Publishers, New York 10016

ILLUSTRATORS

DISTRIBUTORS:

Canada
Saunders of Toronto, Ltd., Don Mills, Ontario

Great Britain and the Commonwealth
Constable & Co., Ltd., 10-12 Orange Street, London WC. 2

Austria, Germany and Switzerland
Arthur Niggli, Ltd., Bohl, 9052 Niederteufen AR, Switzerland

France
Editions Parallèles, 172 rue Pelleport, Paris XXe

Other Countries in Europe
Feffer & Simons, Inc., 696 Keizersgracht, Amsterdam-C, The Netherlands
Latin America, the Orient and Near East
Feffer & Simons, Inc., 31 Union Square, New York 10003

ILLUSTRATORS

CONTENTS

ILLUSTRATORS

PRESIDENT'S MESSAGE

Each year the Society of Illustrators Annual Show gains in stature. Unfortunately it becomes more and more difficult to accept many deserving pieces for the simple reasons of hanging space restrictions in the various galleries, and the limit necessarily made for the reproductions in the published Annual. Here, then, is the thoughtful choice of what we feel to be a cross-section of the best in illustration today.

If you were to look at Volume 1 along with Volume 11, you will surely find the techniques that are worlds apart, and yet see the styles that are ever perennial. "What new approach could there possibly be, now?" we wonder, and yet here again we find a new vitality that will surely inspire another attitude and style another year.

This is why, aside from its historical value, this volume is an important tool in the everyday life of the artist, the buyer and the art student alike.

My thanks to the many stout-hearted individuals who gave their time, talent and unlimited energies to help maintain the high caliber of selections for the Show, and for its preservation in this Volume 11.

WESLEY B. McKEOWN

ILLUSTRATORS

CHAIRMAN'S NOTES

Yes, Virginia, illustration is alive. This show and this book are proof. Illustrators are pushing out. Stretching into new areas of thought and approach, adding new techniques and insights to this venerable old art. Background, middle ground, foreground have given place to concept, relationship, relevance.

To be chairman of this show was an exciting and humbling experience. To watch Illustrators 11 spring from a "Call For Entries" into a full-blown exhibit; to watch the juries choose widely and yet of necessity reject great pieces of work; to see the outstanding work of artists from all parts of the country is almost overwhelming to a chairman who is also an illustrator.

The Illustrators Annuals have almost reached the stage of being an institution, but they can never become square or "establishment" as long as individual illustrators continue to submit their best, their freshest work. If you think the show too conservative or too avant garde, I can only submit that the show is a reflection of the work that was entered.

Many people contributed great efforts selflessly to bring this show into being. As chairman I know there wouldn't be a show without them.

Now Illustrators 11 is a book, a catalog, a record, a reminiscence. Put it on the shelf with your other art books, but look at it occasionally. I am sure you will always find a little something new in it.

CHARLES McVICKER

ILLUSTRATORS

EDITOR'S COMMENT

In working closely with the material in this book, I was strongly moved by the rich diversity of interpretation of visual problems. This diversity is possibly due in part to the daring and experimental approach which is perhaps the distinctive mark of the Illustrators Art of the Swinging Sixties.

I would like to personally thank all those who contributed their prose or their art to this volume. I was most gratified by the magnitude of their response.

HERB MOTT

ILLUSTRATORS

DESIGNER'S STATEMENT

As the designer of Illustrators 11 I have faced the job with mixed emotions. First of all it is quite an overwhelming task but quite an honor to have been asked to do this annual.

The first responsibility of any designer of an Illustrator Annual is to forget personalities and do the layouts as a strict design problem. In compiling this particular volume, which has fewer pages than last year, we had less color pages to work with. This I felt was an unfortunate situation because of the large amount of exceptional color work in this show. However, in deference to the lack of color pages, I have tried to show as many illustrations as large as possible. Working each spread strictly as a value pattern and design element, which changes pace on each spread.

It was my hope in designing Illustrators 11 that it will serve as an accurate record of the illustrations of our times. For I feel that art has value of expressing the temperament of the society in which it reigns. Therefore, I think that future illustrators will be able to refer, in years to come, and benefit from the art displayed between these covers.

I hereby dedicate this volume of Illustrators 11 to my very dear wife Phyllis.

Her death occurred suddenly when this book was nearing completion.

CHARLES LONG

Note:
The medalists and award winners of
ILLUSTRATORS 11 are indicated in the
credits in this Annual as follows:
** GOLD MEDAL
* AWARD FOR EXCELLENCE

JURIES

The Society Of Illustrations Is Indebted To The
Following Distinguished Juries Who Gave Their Time
And Energies In Making The Selections And Awards.

ADVERTISING ILLUSTRATION
George Guzzi, Chairman
Thomas Allen
Samuel Antupit
Harry Bennet
Abril Lamarque
Mary Mayo
Frank McCarthy
Jerry Pinkney
EDITORIAL ILLUSTRATION
Robert Blattner, Chairman
Austin Briggs

Al Catalano
Louis Glanzman
Forbes Linkhorn
Bob Peak
Charles Santore
Miriam Schottland
INSTITUTIONAL ILLUSTRATION
David Passalaqua, Chairman
Lena Bernbom
Harry Carter
Joe DeMers
Phil Hays

Don Hedin
Wilson McLean
Herb Mott
BOOK ILLUSTRATION
Robert Hanoville, Chairman
Bernard D'Andrea
Joan Eby
Bernie Fuchs
Robert Greenwell
Charles Long
Isadore Seltzer
Nicholas Solovioff

COMMITTEE

Chairman
Charles McVicker

Assistant Chairman
Alvin J. Pimsler
Treasurer
Walter Hortens
Annual Editor
Herb Mott
Annual Designer
Charles A. Long
Gallery Committee Chairman
David Stone

Jury Coordinators
Gerald McConnell
Olivia Cole
Barnett Plotkin
Forbes Linkhorn
Shannon Stirnweis
Luncheon Chairman
Harry Carter
Hanging Committee
Mitchell Hooks
Carl McVicker

Office Staff
Arpi Ermoyan
Elaine Samperi
Gladys Tashian

BARYE

This past year saw the untimely death of Baryé Winchell Phillips, recent past president for two years of the Society of Illustrators.

Baryé began his schooling at a youthful 14 at the Art Students League and at the National Academy of Fine Arts. From there began a lifetime career in illustration that covered all areas of design and painting from the movie industry through the various phases of the book publishing world.

He was greatly respected for his versatility of style in his professional work and for the freedom and freshness of his paintings. He loved his work, and it showed.

No member of the Society can forget his warm, easygoing, unaffected manner.

He is missed.

ILLUSTRATORS

A FRAME FOR THE PICTURE

Last minute adjustments were made in the new lighting. Oversize floral arrangements were added, ash trays placed, a few frames straightened and — the transformation was complete.

The first show had been hung in the Society of Illustrators beautiful new gallery and the tale that follows is of how this came to be.

THE HIGH COST OF EXHIBITING

It all began when some of the members were planning a group exhibition in the main floor gallery at S.I. Plans had been worked out to display a well rounded, highly representative show of illustration with emphasis on quality of work and taste in exhibition. The primary obstacle was the forlorn state of the gallery. No matter the form taken by the art to be hung, whether traditional in scope or radical in nature, it was recognized that a great deal of importance lay in the surroundings to display the work at its finest.

When the ten artists began to count up the costs of disguising the falling-down ceiling, covering the dingy and battered walls, screening the dilapidated stage, augmenting the antique wiring and lighting, patching the occasionally missing linoleum flooring — they nearly forgot the whole idea.

THE EMERGENCY WAS CLEAR

At approximately the same time the Annual Exhibition Committee came up with a dandy crisis. The expected midtown show space — suddenly became unavailable. In past years it had been the S.I. custom to display the exhibition of over 400 pieces first in our own gallery and then move the entire show to a midtown location, nearer art purchasing centers. The emergency was clear and so were the alternatives. The fees charged exhibitors could be increased to cover a large rental payment for a midtown exhibition area or — hang the art in our own gallery on the edge of the advertising, publishing district.

The nod fell to the home show providing something could be done for the shoddy old showroom. Illustrators 11 was scheduled for January 20, less than two months away. A volunteer task force took on the responsibility of giving birth to the new gallery. To design a room for a group of bankers or lawyers would be difficult enough but for 500 artists, all master designers, this presented a somewhat larger problem.

Preliminary investigations only proved this problem to be even larger than anticipated. After a number of false starts the project was turned over to architect Kan Domoto who performed miracles with our limited budget. With the faith of the innocent the committee ordered work to proceed.

THE DEADLY DEADLINE

Illustrators are familiar with deadlines and often thrive on them, but when a tight schedule is cut in half. The film company 20th Century Fox petitioned to film a scene from the John McDermott story "Brooks Wilson, Ltd." in our new gallery to be before the annual exhibition! Carpenters swarmed over the old gallery putting up new walls and carpeting them, the stage was incorporated into the larger exhibition area, and a cleverly designed ceiling grill of raw lumber concealed the ancient ceiling and wall lighting. A handsome gray carpet covered the floor. Fixtures were added and details painted. Two dozen members moved in at the last minute to complete the finishing touches and the remodeling was complete.

THOSE WHO MADE IT POSSIBLE

The new gallery was achieved by the efforts of a few artists and financing from a large number of contributors. Grateful acknowledgement for financial contribution is made to:

The Readers Digest Foundation
Mrs. De Witt Wallace
McCalls Corporation
Arthur William Brown
Museum of Illustration Art
Estelle Mandel
Annual National Exhibition Account
Society of Illustrators Inc.

Some of the S.I. services that will be directly benefited each year are:

The Annual National Illustrators Exhibition
Exhibits from Allied Organizations
Individual and group exhibits
The National Student Competition
The Warwick Boys School Show
The U.S. Air Force Exhibition
The U.S. Parks Department Exhibition

Grateful acknowledgement for the physical contribution of the Gallery Improvement Task Force is made to:

D. K. Stone
Arpi Ermoyan
Gerald McConnell
Robert Geissmann
Walter Brooks
Donald Moss
Donald Smith
Andrew Tanuma

and the great number of members who backed their advice with help when asked.

DAVID K. STONE

THEDORE CROSLIN

"Teddy"

In 1968 the members of the Society of Illustrators were profoundly saddened by the death of our club steward "Teddy." Each of us who were fortunate to know him, a gentle and wonderful person, feel our own personal sense of loss. We all experienced first hand his special quality of making you feel welcome and at home whether you were a member, a guest, a visitor or a young student in our gallery.

The rest of this salute to Teddy is from Harold Von Schmidt. I sat with Von on an August afternoon. Von looked back upon the time in 1931, when as president of the Society in our former building on 24th Street, he hired Teddy.

"I told Teddy then that his most important function in his new job was to make the club a friendly place where everyone would want to come and enjoy themselves. This Teddy has done. Through the years his brand of hospitality and devotion enriched all of us.

My last visit with Teddy was here at my home in Westport at my 75th Birthday Barbecue. Teddy drove out from New York City with Frank Wilbright. The party ended with a late bull session in my kitchen with Frank and Teddy. It was a happy hour of remembering many occasions of human pleasure and friendship.

We will all miss Teddy. His greatest contribution was that he liked people.

Being hospitalized myself at the time of Teddy's death, I was comforted to know that a chartered bus was filled with members of the Society who rode out to attend his last rites held across the East River in a Long Island church. I wish I could have been there too."

Teddy's presence and influence continues in our memories and inspires us to contribute our share to human fellowship.

STEVAN DOHANOS
August 19, 1969

2
Book
Artist: **Jerry Pinkney**
Art Director: **Morris Kerchoff**
Publisher: **Allyn & Bacon, Inc.**

3
Advertising
Artist: Jerry Pinkney
Art Director: Edward Russell
Client: Champion Papers

4
Book
Artist: George Sottung

5
Editorial
Artist: Hans Falk
Art Director: Walter Allner
Publication: Fortune Magazine

6
Editorial
Artist: David Noyes
Art Director: Richard Gangel
Publication: Sports Illustrated

7
Book
Artist: Jerry Pinkney
Art Director: Morris Kerchoff
Publisher: Allyn & Bacon, Inc.

8
Editorial
Artist: **Herb Davidson**
Art Director: **Arthur Paul**
Publication: **Playboy Magazine**

9
Book
Artist: **Robert Baxter**
Art Director: **Ken Hine/Donald Hedin**
Publisher: **Reader's Digest Books**

10
Institutional
Artist: **Bill Brewer**
Art Director: **Bill Brewer**
Client: **Buzza-Cardozo**

11
Institutional
Artist: **John Alcorn**
Art Director: **Tony Russell/Kit Hinrichs**
Agency: **Russell & Hinrichs Associates**
Client: **Chase Manhattan Bank**

12
Institutional
Artist: **Dick Brown**
Art Director: **Gary Shinn**
Client: **Seattle Art Directors Society**

13
Editorial
Artist: Garie Blackwell
Art Director: Herb Bleiweiss/Bruce Danbrot
Publication: Ladies' Home Journal

14
Editorial
Artist: **Gary Lund**
Art Director: **Lowell Butler**
Publication: **Westways Magazine**

1
Editoria
Artist: **Paul Davi**
Art Director: **Kenneth Munowit**
Publication: **Horizon Magazin**

PAINTING BY GARY LUND

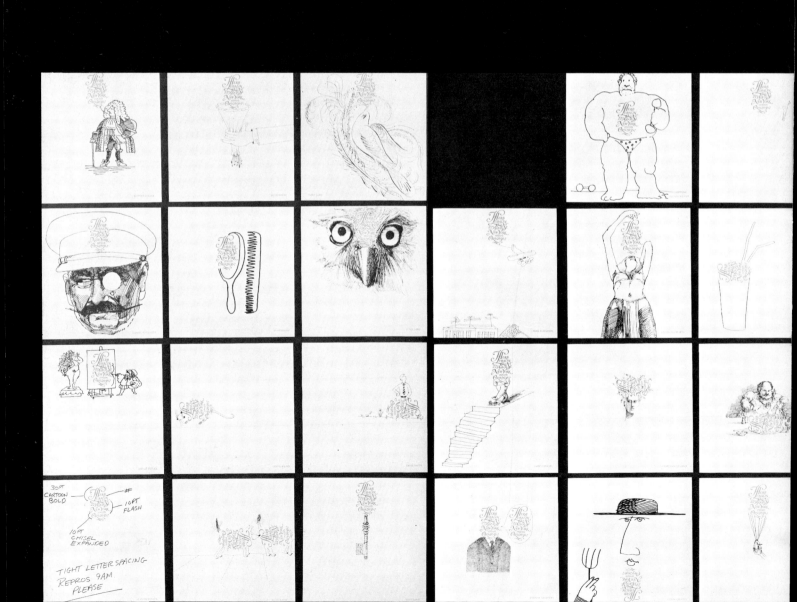

18

19
Institutional
Artist: **Herb Lubalin, Inc.**
Art Director: **Ernie Smith**
Client: **Herb Lubalin, Inc.**

20
Book
Artist: Jerry Pinkney
Art Director: Morris Kerchoff
Publisher: Allyn & Bacon, Inc.

21
Book
Artist: Ed Aitchison
Art Director: Hal Kearney
Publisher: Scott Foresman & Co.

Pass the Lord and
PRAISE THE AMMUNITIO

23
Editorial
Artist: Bill Utterback
Art Director: Arthur Paul
Publication: Playboy Magazine

2
Institutional
Artist: Edward Sorel
Art Director: Edward Sorel
Client: Edward Sorel

24
Institutional
Artist:
Reynold Ruffins/Simms Taback
Art Director:
Reynold Ruffins/Simms Taback
Client:
Ruffins/Taback, Inc

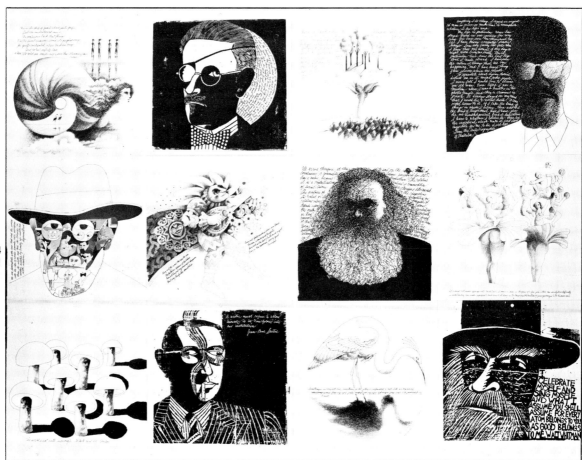

27
Editorial
Artist: **Bill Charmatz**
Art Director: **Richard Gangel**
Publication: **Sports Illustrated**

25
Editorial
Artist: **Domenico Gnoli**
Art Director: **Walter Allner**
Publication: **Fortune Magazine**

26
Book
Artist: **Edward Gorey**
Art Director: **Hilda Scott**
Publisher: **Holt, Rinehart & Winston, Inc.**

28
Institutional
Artist: **Don Weller**

29
Institutional
Artist: **Lorraine Fox**

30
Advertising
Artist: Paul Calle
Art Director: Eugene Kolomatsky
Client: N. B. C.

31
Book
Artist: James Barkley
Art Director: Lynn Hatfield
Publisher: Dell Publishing Co.

32
Advertising
Artist: Gene Szafran
Art Director: Bill Harvey
Client: Elektra Records

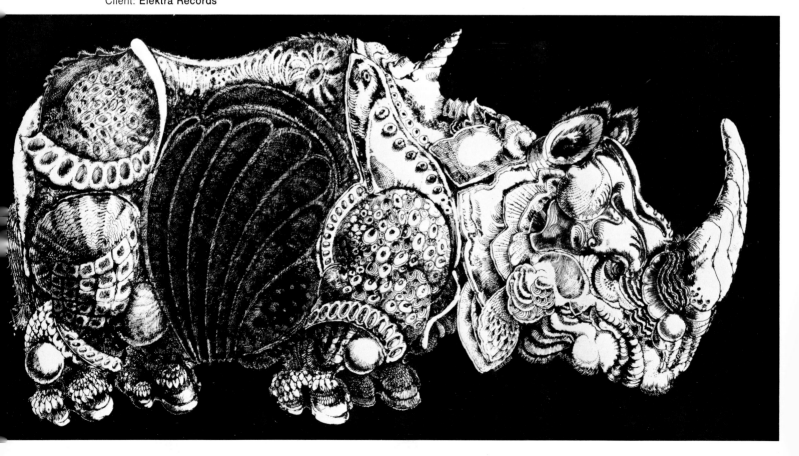

33
Book
Artist: **Jim Spanfeller**
Art Director: **Bob Cheney**
Publisher: **Harper & Row**

34
Editorial
Artist: **James Cooper**
Art Director: **Judi Parker**
Publication: **Eye Magazine**

Strength

The Magician

The Emperor

The Lovers

The Fool

eye

High Priestess

The Hermit

Judgment

Temperance

Wheel of Fortune

Death

The Star

The Empress

The Moon

Hanged Man

Justice

The World

ariot

The Hierophant

The Tower

35
Institutional
Artist: **Lorraine Fox**

36
Advertising
Artist: **Charles Slackman**
Art Director: **Irving Cowman**
Agency: **Young & Rubicam, Inc.**
Client: **Eastern Airlines**

37
Editorial
Artist: Robert Brickhouse

38
Institutional
Artist: **Ted Coconis**
Art Director: **Charles Volpe**
Client: **World Art Group**

39
Editorial
Artist: **Barrington Smith**

41
Institutional
Artist: **Kit Hinrichs**
Art Director: **Tony Russell/Kit Hinrichs**
Agency: **Russell & Hinrichs Associates**
Client: **Chase Manhattan Bank**

40
Advertising
Artist: **James Jebavy**
Art Director: **Robert Pearson**
Agency: **Higgens, Hegner & Genovese, Inc.**
Client: **United Airlines, Inc.**

42

45

42
Editorial
Artist: David Johnson
Art Director: Lene Bernbom
Publication: Cosmopolitan Magazine

43
Advertising
Artist: Ted DeBosier
Art Director: Henry Epstein
Client: ABC Television

44
Institutional
Artist: Jack Endewelt
Art Director: Ken Sneider/Murray Miller
Publisher: Reader's Digest

45
Editorial
Artist: Tom Lovell
Art Director: Andrew Poggenpohl
Publication: National Geographic Society

46
Advertising
Artist: Sam Cooperstein
Art Director: Bernie Zlotnick
Agency: Young & Rubicam, Inc.
Client: Pioneer Moss

43

46

44

47
Institutional
Artist: Ken Dallison
Art Director: Tom McLaine
Client: B. F. Goodrich Co.

49
Editorial
Artist: Alex Gnidziejko
Art Director: Ulrich Boege
Publication: Status Magazine

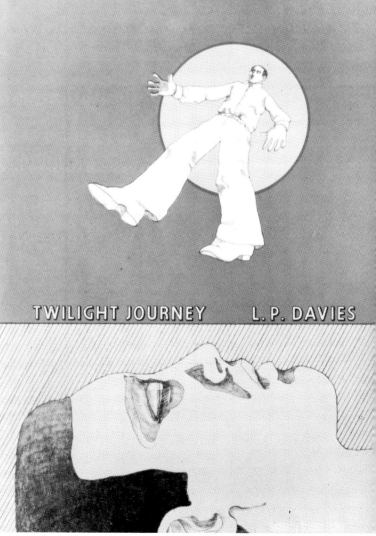

TWILIGHT JOURNEY   L. P. DAVIES

50
Book
Artist: Emanuel Schongut
Art Director: Margo Herr
Publisher: Doubleday & Co.

48
Advertising
Artist: Gerry Gersten
Art Director: Emmet McBane
Agency: Klemtner Agency
Client: Pfizer Pharmaceutical

51
Editorial
Artist: Doug Johnson
Art Director: Joan Fenton
Publication: Seventeen Magazine

52
Book
Artist: Robert Baxter
Art Director: Ken Hine/Donald Hedin
Publisher: Reader's Digest Books

53
Book
Artist: Gyo Fujikawa
Art Director: Archie Bennett
Publisher: Grosset & Dunlap

54
Book
Artist: John Burningham
Art Director: Allen Carr
Publisher: Follett Publishing Co.

55
Advertising
Artist: Alvin Pimsler
Art Director: Martin Stevens
Client: Revlon, Inc.

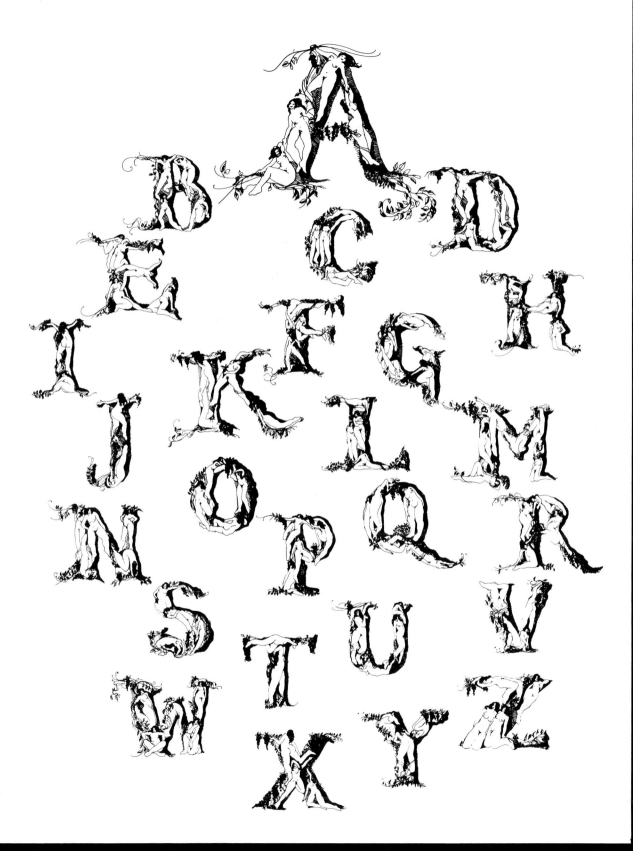

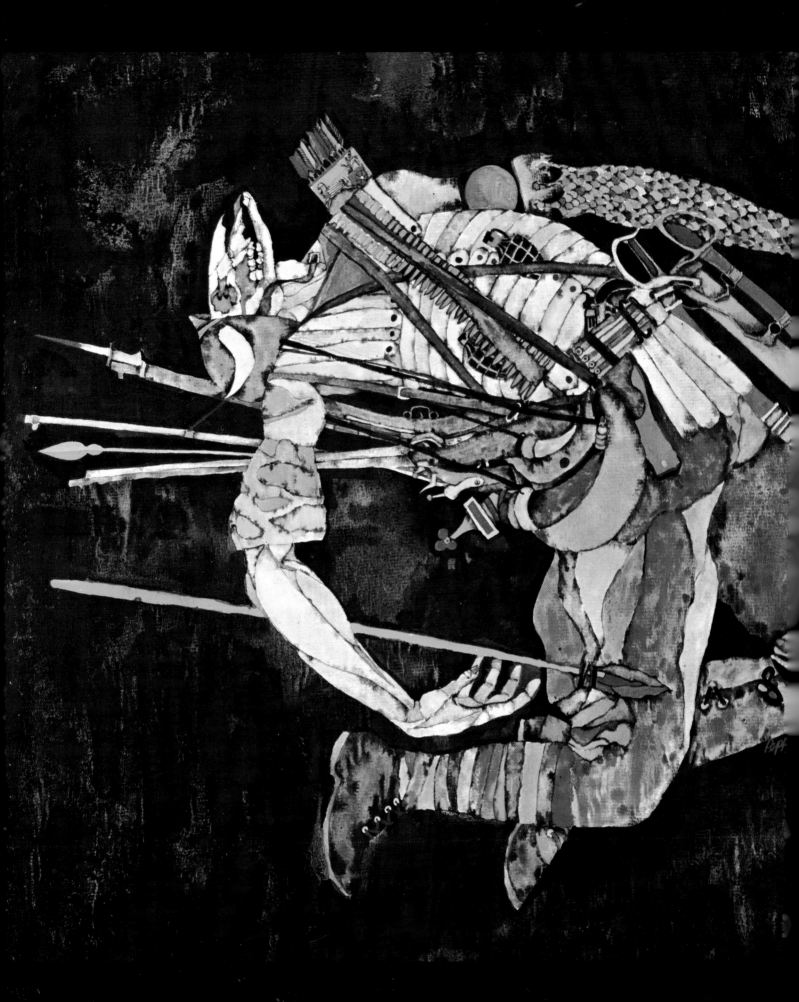

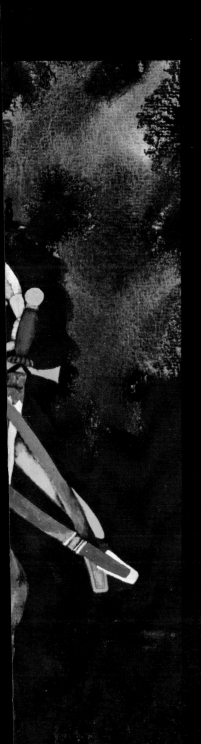

58
Book
Artist: **Bill Greer**
Art Director: **Harald Peter**
Publisher: **Hallmark Cards, Inc.**

59
Editorial
Artist: **Milton Glaser**
Art Director: **Dugald Stermer**
Publication: **Ramparts Magazine**

57
Advertising
Artist: **Bob Pepper**
Art Director: **Bill Harvey**
Client: **Nonesuch Records**

60
Book
Artist: **John Huehnergarth**
Art Director: **Zelda Haber**
Publisher: **Crowell-Collier Educational Corp.**

63
Editorial
Artist: **Joe Isom**
Art Director: **Arthur Paul**
Publication: **Playboy Magazine**

61
Institutional
Artist: **Herb Tauss**
Client: **U.S. Air Force**

62
Book
Artist: **Joe Isom**
Art Director: **Harald Peter**
Client: **Hallmark Cards, Inc.**

64
Book
Artist: **Ed Aitchison**
Art Director: **Hal Kearney**
Publisher: **Scott Foresman & Co.**

66
Institutional
Artist: **Robert A. Parker**
Art Director: **Richard Wachter**
Agency: **L. W. Frohlich & Co.**
Client: **CIBA**

65
Institutional
Artist: **Merv Corning**
Art Director: **Hy Yablanca**
Agency: **Jay Chiat & Assoc.**
Client: **Leach Corp.**

67
Editorial
Artist: **James Wyeth**
Art Director: **Allen Hurlburt**
Publication: **Look** Magazine

68
Book
Artist: **Ron Bradford**
Art Director: **Hal Kearney**
Publisher: **Scott Foresman & Co.**

69
Institutional
Artist: Ron Wolin

70
Book
Artist: Frank Cannas
Art Director: Harold Evans
Publisher: Holt, Rinehart & Winston, Inc.

73
Editorial
Artist: Gerry Gersten
Art Director: Murray Belsky
Publication: American Heritage Magazin

72
Advertising
Artist: Bob Peak
Art Director: Windsor Mallett
Agency: B.B.D.O., Boston
Client: S. D. Warren Co.

71
Book
Artist: Phil Renaud
Art Director: Hal Kearney
Publisher: Scott Foresman & Co.

74

77
Editorial
Artist: Murray Tinkelman
Art Director: Andy Lessin
Publication: Boy's Life Magazine

74
Editorial
Artist: Hedda
Art Director: Desmond English
Publication: MacClean's Magazine

75
Advertising
Artist: Murray Tinkelman

76
Editorial
Artist: Gilbert L. Stone
Art Director: Joan Fenton
Publication: Seventeen Magazine

75

76

79
Editorial
Artist: Bernie Fuchs
Art Director: Kirk Wilkinson
Publication: Women's Day Magazine

78
Advertising
Artist: **Gene Szafran**
Art Director: **Bill Harvey**
Client: **Elektra Records**

80
Advertising
Artist: **Frank Bozzo**
Art Director: **William Harvey**
Client: **Nonesuch Records**

83 Book   Artist: **George Roth**   Art Director: **Hal Kearney**   Publisher: **Scott Foresman & Co.**

IN FLANDERS FIELDS

John McCrae
1872-1918

In Flanders fields the poppies blow
Between the crosses, row on row,
That mark our place; and in the sky
The larks, still bravely singing, fly
Scarce heard amid the guns below.

We are the Dead. Short days ago
We lived, felt dawn, saw sunset glow,
Loved and were loved and now we lie
    In Flanders fields.

Take up our quarrel with the foe;
To you from failing hands we throw
The torch; be yours to hold it high.
If ye break faith with us who die
We shall not sleep, though poppies grow
    In Flanders fields.

stitutional
st: Charles Passarelli
Director: Bradley L. Wilson
ent: General Electric Co.

84
Institutional
Artist: Bart Forbes
Art Director: Bart Forbes
Publisher: Heritage Press

stitutional
tist: Marvin Mattelson

86
Editorial
Artist: Alan E. Cober
Art Director: Andrew Lessin
Publication: Boy's Life Magazine

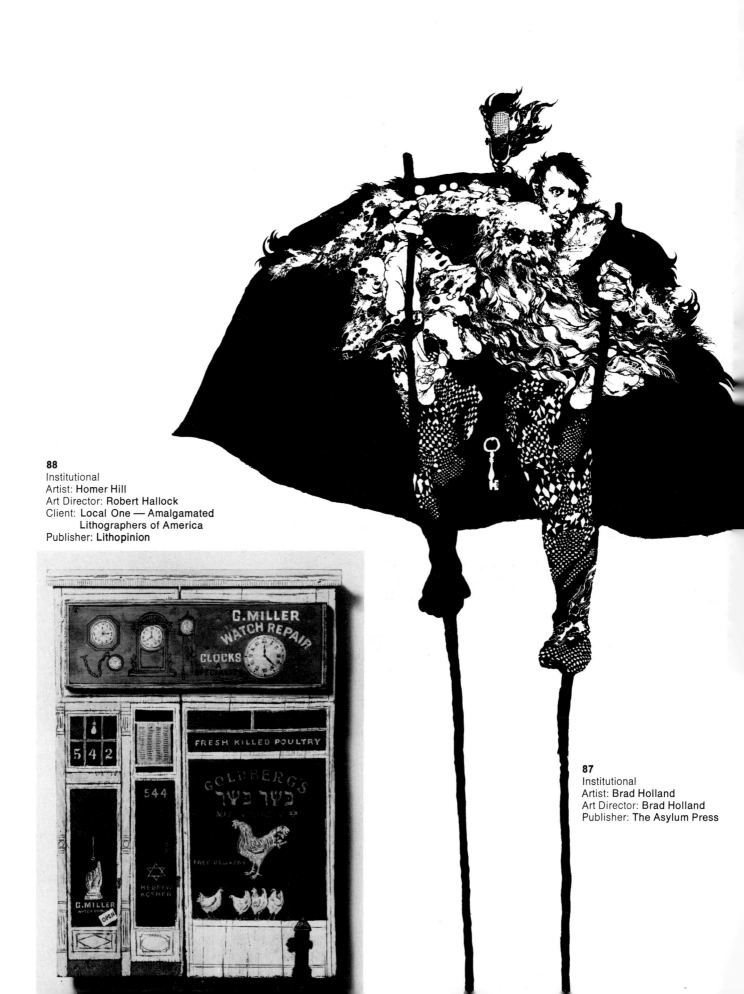

88
Institutional
Artist: Homer Hill
Art Director: Robert Hallock
Client: Local One — Amalgamated
             Lithographers of America
Publisher: Lithopinion

87
Institutional
Artist: Brad Holland
Art Director: Brad Holland
Publisher: The Asylum Press

89
Editorial
Artist: **Bob Peak**
Art Director: **Andrew Lessin**
Publication: **Boy's Life Magazine**

90
Advertising:
Artist: **Charles Santore**
Art Director: **Richard Herdegan**
Client: **Avril Rayon**

91

92

95

93

94

96

91
Institutional
Artist: Tom Ballenger

92
Advertising
Artist: Margaret Howlett
Art Director: Russell D'Anna
Publisher: Scholastic Books

93
Editorial
Artist: Arthur Shilstone
Art Director: Reg Massie
Publication: The Reporter

94
Book
Artist: Phero Thomas
Art Director: Hal Kearney
Publisher: Scott Foresman & Co.

95
Editorial
Artist: Chuck Wilkinson
Art Director: Herb Bleiweiss/Bruce Danbrot
Publication: Ladies' Home Journal

96
Institutional
Artist: Paul Williams

97
Editorial
Artist: **Mark English**
Art Director: **Herb Bleiweiss/Bruce Danbrot**
Publication: **Ladies' Home Journal**

98
Advertising
Artist: **Victor Atkins**
Art Director: **John Berg**
Client: **Columbia Records**

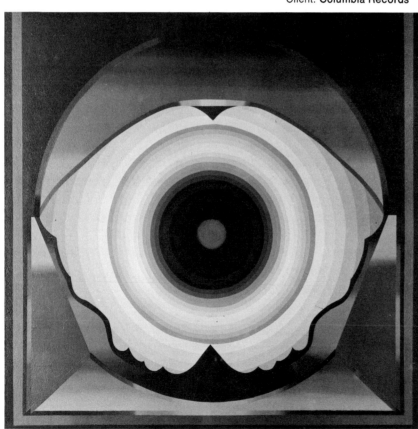

99
Institutional
Artist: **Don E. Dubowski**
Art Director: **Jeannette Lee**
Client: **Hallmark Cards, Inc.**

100
Institutional
Artist: Donald M. Hedin
Client: U.S. Air Force

101

101
Advertising
Artist: James Jebavy
Art Director: James Lavengood
Agency: Higgens, Hegner & Genovese, Inc
Client: United Airlines, Inc.

104
Editorial
Artist: Joseph Modica

102
Institutional
Artist: Barnett Plotkin

103
Advertising
Artist: Robert Lockhart
Art Director: George Osaki
Client: Capitol Records

104

105
Advertising
Artist: **Joe Isom**
Client: **Glenn Printing Co.**

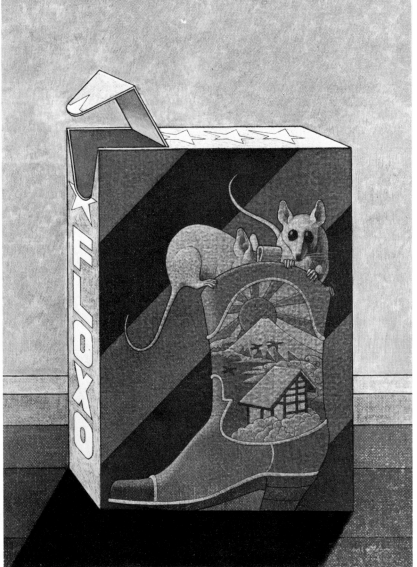

107
Editorial
Artist: **Don Ivan Punchatz**
Art Director: **Arthur Paul**
Publication: **Playboy Magazine**

108
Editorial
Artist: **Mark English**
Art Director: **Herb Bleiweiss/Bruce Danbrot**
Publication: **Ladies' Home Journal**

106
Advertising
Artist: **Arthur Shilstone**

109
Book
Artist: Peter Caras
Art Director: George Paturzo
Publisher: Berkeley Books

110
Institutional
Artist: John Scott Overmeyer
Art Director: Rick Lyons
Client: Hallmark Cards, Inc.

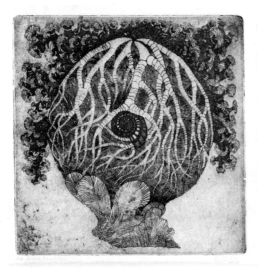
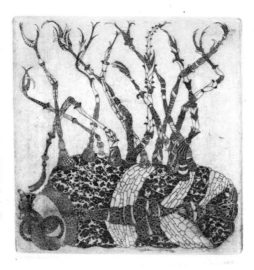

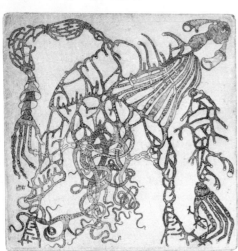
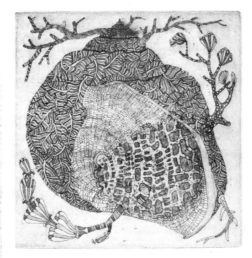
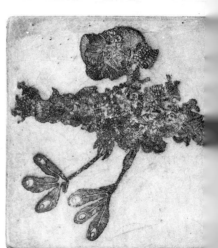

112
Book
Artist: John Trotta
Art Director: Harald Peter
Client: Hallmark Cards, Inc.

111
Advertising
Artist: Wolfgang Walther
Art Director: Jaques Hauser
Agency: F. Hoffmann LaRoche & Co.

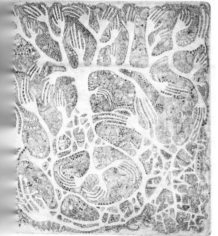

113
Book
Artist: Evaline Ness
Art Director: Hilda Scott
Publisher: Holt, Rinehart & Winston, Inc.

114
Book
Artist: Leona Wood
Art Director: Ken Hine/Donald Hedin
Book Title: Best Loved Books #7
Publisher: Reader's Digest Books

115
Institutional
Artist: Robert Heindel
Art Director: Gery Colby
Agency: James Dunn & Assoc.
Client: Detroit Red Wings

THE RUSSIAN LESSON

DESIGNED FOR YOUR EDIFICATION, ENLIGHTENMENT AND ENTERTAINMENT

НАУ́КА
Nahookah (Science)

ЛЮБО́ВЬ
Lyoubohv (Love)

ПИТЬЁ
Peetyuh (Drink)

МЕДВЕ́ДЬ Myehdvehdh (Bear)

СНЕГ
Snyehg (Snow)

БАБОЧКА
Bahbohchkah (Butterfly)

ДЕД
Dyehd (Grandfather)

СИ́МБОЛ
Seembohl (Symbol)

БИ́ТВА
Beetvah (Battle)

ЛО́ДКА
Lohdkah (Boat)

ОПРОКИ́ДЫВАТЬ
Oprokeedihvaht (Overturn)

ЗВЕЗДА́
Zvezdah (Star)

ЗМЕЯ́
Zmeyah (Snake)

КОСОГЛА́ЗЫЙ
Kosoglazihee (Crosseyed)

НОС
Nohs (Nose)

ВЕ́ЕР
Vyeiyehr (Fan)

ПИ́ЩА
Peestchah (Food)

РУ́ССКИЙ УРО́К

Designed by LIONEL KALISH/Produced by CULLEN RAPP STUDIOS, 251 East 51 Street, New York, N.Y. 10022

116
Institutional
Artist: Lionel Kalish
Art Director: Lionel Kalish
Client: Sanders Printing Co.

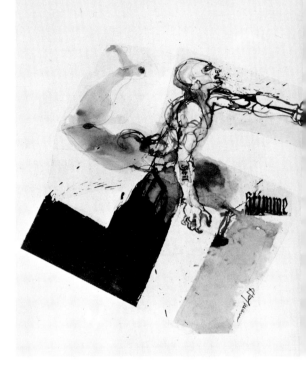

117
Institutional
Artist: **Paul Calle**
Art Director: **Stewart Bennion**
Client: **The Garrett Corp., Inc.**

118
Book
Artist: **William Hofmann**
Art Director: **Leonard Leone**
Publisher: **Bantam Books, Inc.**

121

120
Advertising
Artist: **Paul Davis**
Art Director: **Robert Defrin**
Client: **R.C.A. Records**

122

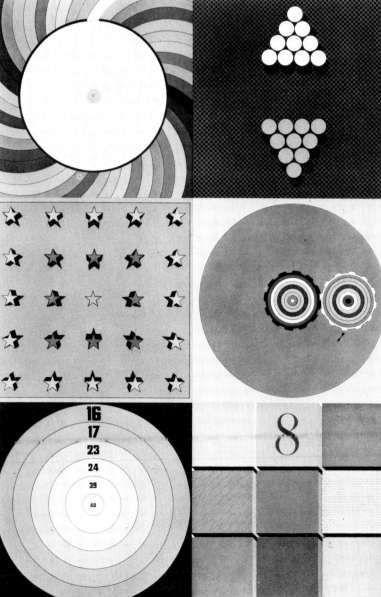

19

9
torial
st: Edward Sorel
Director: Samuel Antupit
lication: Esquire Magazine

torial
st: Donald Moss
Director: Richard Gangel
lication: Sports Illustrated

itutional
st: Isadore Seltzer
Director: Isadore Seltzer
nt: Harvey Kahn Associates

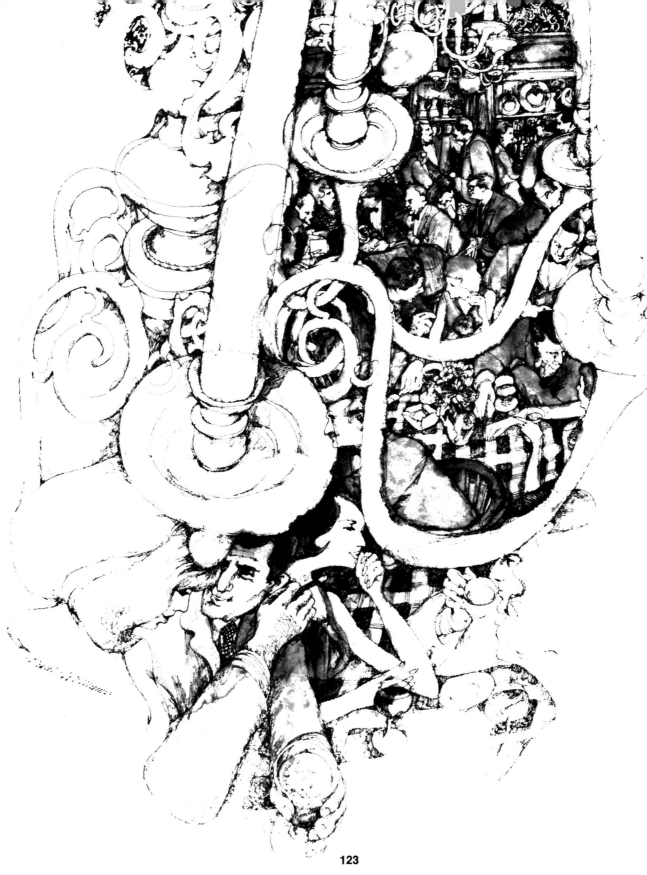

123

123
Advertising
Artist: Paul Williams

124
Editorial
Artist: Marvin Hayes
Art Director: Arthur Paul
Publication: Playboy Magazine

125
Editorial
Artist: Milton Glaser
Art Director: Bernard Quint
Publication: Life Magazine

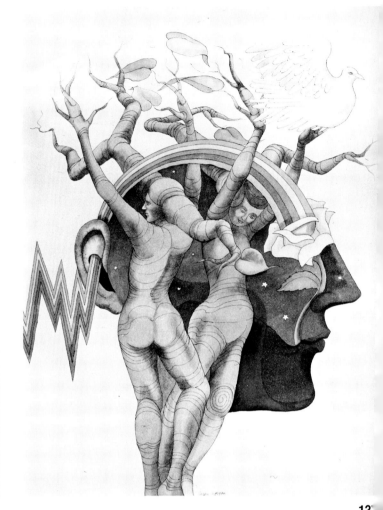

126
Book
Artist: **Jerry Helmrich**

127
Advertising
Artist: **Jacqui Morgan**
Art Director: **Phil Schulman**
Agency: **N. W. Ayer & Son**
Client: **American Telephone & Telegraph Co.**

128
Advertising
Artist: **Bob Peak**
Art Director: **Robert Forgione**
Agency: **William Esty Co.**
Client: **Reynolds Tobacco Co.**

129
Editorial
Artist: **Paul Davis**
Art Director: **Kenneth Deardoff**
Publication: **Evergreen Review**

130
Book
Artist: **Victor Valla**

128

129

131
Advertising
Artist: Robert A. Parker
Art Director: John Berg
Client: Columbia Records

132
Editorial
Artist: Isadore Seltzer
Art Director: Alvin Grossman
Publication: Venture Magazine

134
Book
Artist: Richard Schlecht
Art Director: Joseph Taney
Publisher: National Geographic Society

My octopus has many hands;
He holds my lollipops.
And sometimes for my mother
He carries pails and mops.

133
Book
Artist: **Ed Renfro**
Art Director: **Alan Heicklen**
Publisher: **Holt, Rinehart & Winston, Inc.**

135
Editorial
Artist: **Paul Jasmin**
Art Director: **Sam Antupit**
Publication: **Esquire Magazine**

135

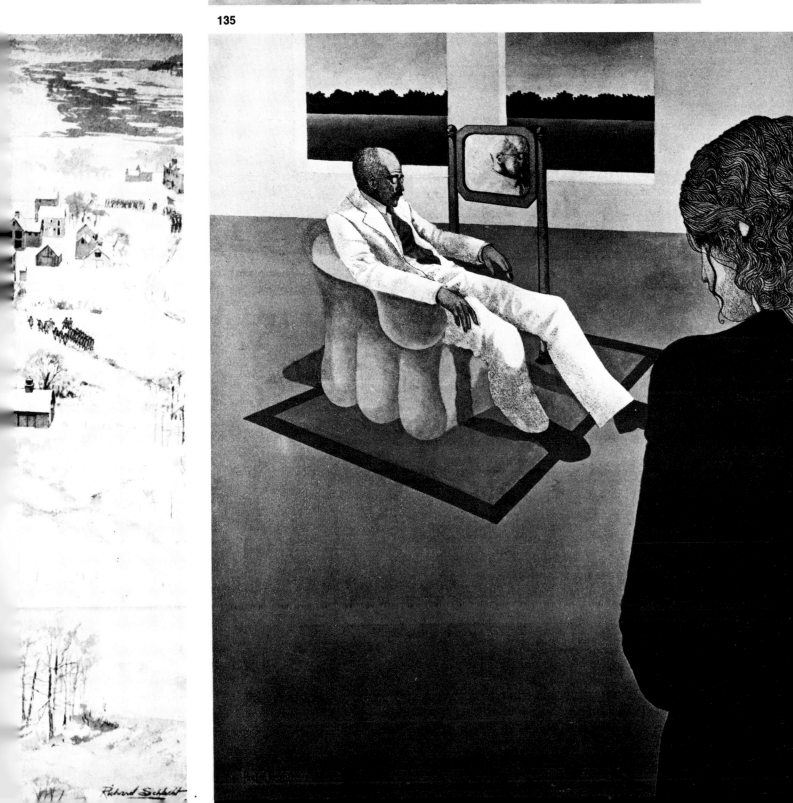

136
Advertising
Artist: **Marvin Friedman**
Art Director: **John Graham**
Client: **N.B.C.**

137
Editorial
Artist: **Bernie Fuchs**
Art Director: **William Hopkins**
Publication: **Look Magazine**

138
Advertising
Artist: **Seymour Chwast**
Art Director: **Seymour Chwast**
Client: **Famous Faces**

End Bad Breath.

139
Institutional
Artist: Isadore Seltzer
Art Director: Howard Menken/Abe Seltzer/
    Phil Fiorello
Agency: R. E. Wilson
Client: Eaton Laboratories

140
Institutional
Artist: Jack N. Unruh
Art Director: George Buckow
Publisher: Houston Post

142
Book
Artist: Milton Charles
Art Director: Leonard Leone
Publisher: Bantam Books, Inc.

143
Editorial
Artist: Daniel Schwartz
Art Director: Samuel Antupit
Publication: Esquire Magazine

141
Institutional
Artist: Richard Hess
Art Director: Richard Hess
Client: Key Note Promotions, Inc.

They don't do anything.

Sales aids should sell.

to show you what we can do,
n't be bored.   LE 2-7680

Keynote Promotions

144
Advertising
Artist: **Jacqui Morgan**
Art Director: **Onnig Kalfayan**
Agency: **Onnig, Inc.**
Client: **Celanese Corp.**

145
Book
Artist: **Alex Gnidziejko**
Art Director: **Russ D'Anna**
Publisher: **Scholastic Books**

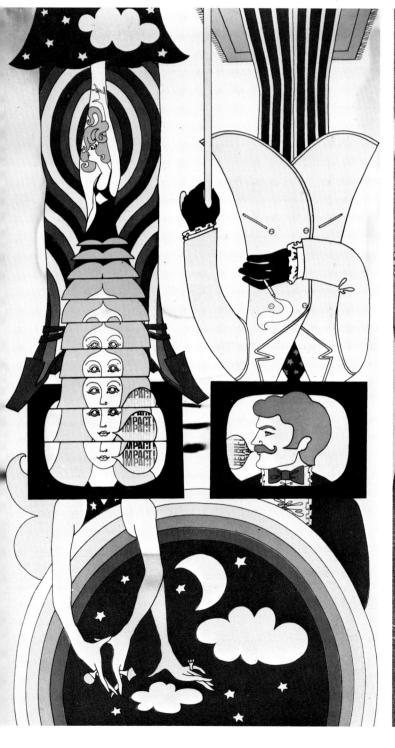

Jackie Gleason
The Now Sound...For Today's Lovers

STEREO
PLAYABLE ON
STEREO & MONO
PHONOGRAPHS

Gleason Strings
and other
exotic instruments

My Head
Yesterday
It Must Be Him
Live for Life
Lonely Is the Name
Can't Take My Eyes Off You
Moon River
Two Different Worlds
I Won't Cry Anymore
I Can't Believe I'm Losing You

149
Book
Artist: **Arnold Lobel**
Art Director: **Dorothy Hagen**
Publisher: **Harper & Row**

147
Editorial
Artist: **Charles McVicker**
Art Director: **Forbes Linkhorn**
Publication: **American Journal of Nursing**

148
Editorial
Artist: **David Negron**

150
Advertising
Artist: Robert Lockhart
Art Director: George Osaki
Client: Capitol Records

151
Editorial
Artist: Marie Michal

153
Book
Artist: Ezra Jack Keats
Art Director: Dorothy Hagen
Publisher: Harper & Row

152
Book
Artist: Stan Hunter
Art Director: Russ D'Anna
Publisher: Scholastic Books

154
Editorial
Artist: **Daniel Maffia**
Art Director: **Joan Fenton**
Publication: **Seventeen Magazine**

155
Institutional
Artist: **Donald M. Hedin**

156
Advertising
Artist: **John Alcorn**
Art Director: Eli Rosenthal
Agency: **B.B.D.O., Inc.**
Client: **B.B.D.O., Inc.**

157
Editorial
Artist: **Austin Briggs**
Art Director: **Allen Hurlburt**
Publication: **Look Magazine**

RF VIET NAM

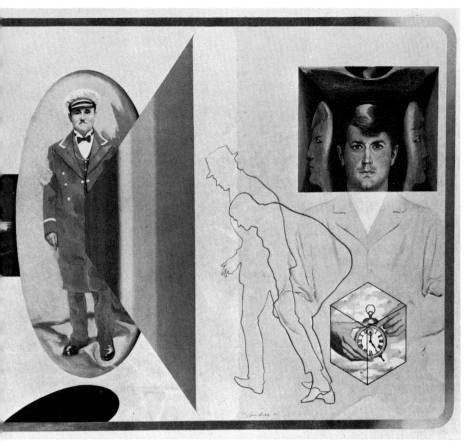

158
Advertising
Artist: **Bernard D'Andrea**

159
Editorial
Artist: **Leo Monahan**
Art Director: **Lowell Butler**
Publication: **Westways Magazine**

160
Advertising
Artist: **Charles Slackman**
Art Director: **Irving Cowman**
Agency: **Young & Rubicam, Inc.**
Client: **Eastern Airlines**

161
Editorial
Artist: **Mark English**
Art Director: **Herb Bleiweiss/Bruce Danbrot**

162
Editorial
Artist: **Tom Lovell**
Art Director: **Andrew Poggenpohl**
Publisher: **National Geographic Society**

164
Editorial
Artist: **C. C. Beall**
Art Director: **Norman Kent**
Publication: **American Artist Magazine**

163
Editorial
Artist: **Carl Owens**
Art Director: **Mort Persky**
Publication: **Detroit Free Press**

165

166

165
Institutional
Artist: William Steig
Art Director: Howard Munce
Client: American Airlines

166
Editorial
Artist: James Hill
Art Director: William Cadge
Publication: Redbook Magazine

167
Book
Artist: Alice and Martin Provensen
Art Director: Carlo DeLucia
Publisher: Western Publishing Co.

168
Advertising
Artist: Raymond Ameijide
Art Director: Robert Defrin
Client: R. C. A. Victor

BILLY THE KID

His real name was William Bonney and, strange as it may seem, his birthplace was New York City. But he became the terror of the West as "Billy the Kid," a nickname that everyone feared. It was said that by the time he had reached twenty-one he had killed a man for each year of his life.

We see him first as a twelve-year-old boy in a frontier town. With his mother he watches cowboys gathering in front of a saloon while a few women from across the border do a Mexican dance called a *jarabe*. Some of the men have been drinking and a quarrel breaks out. The bickering grows into

a brawl and, in the commotion, the Kid's mother is shot. As she falls, the Kid snatches a knife and stabs his mother's slayer. His days as a desperado have begun.

A few years later he is known throughout the land as "The Bad Man of Lincoln County." He defies the law, shoots his way out of every trap set for him, and, unlike Robin Hood who robbed the rich to give to the poor, he steals from everyone at the point of a gun.

His career does not last long. His downfall starts when he is caught cheating at cards by Pat Garrett, one of his pals.

167

168

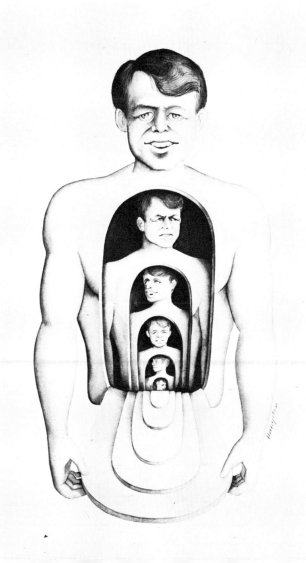

169
Editorial
Artist: Blake Hampton
Art Director: Norman Schoenfeld
Publication: True Magazine

170

170
Editorial
Artist: **Robert Abbett**
Art Director: **Kenneth Stuart**
Publication: **Reader's Digest**

171
Editorial
Artist: **Mark English**
Art Director: **Pasquale Del Vecchio/
          Werner Kappes**
Publication: **McCall's Magazine**

171

174
Book
Artist: **William Vucksonovich**
Art Director: **Allen Carr**
Publisher: **Follett Publishing Co.**

172
Book
Artist: James Hill
Art Director: David Glixon
Publisher: Limited Editions Club

175
Book
Artist: Jim Spanfeller
Art Director: Bob Ramsay
Client: Smith, Kline & French
Publisher: Emphasis Magazine

173
Book
Artist: Ted Lewin
Art Director: Kay Ward/Kenneth Sneider
Publisher: Reader's Digest

Norman Rockwell

177
Advertising
Artist: **Cal Sacks**
Art Director: **John Graham**
Client: **N.B.C.**

178
Advertising
Artist: **Milton Glaser**
Art Director: **John Berg**
Client: **Columbia Records**

179
Editorial
Artist: **Robert Weaver**
Art Director: **Arthur Paul**
Publication: **Playboy Magazine**

180
Institutional
Artist: **Ted Coconis**

181
Book
Artist: **David Negron**

182
Book
Artist: **William Pene du Bois**
Art Director: **Dorothy Hagen**
Publisher: **Harper & Row**

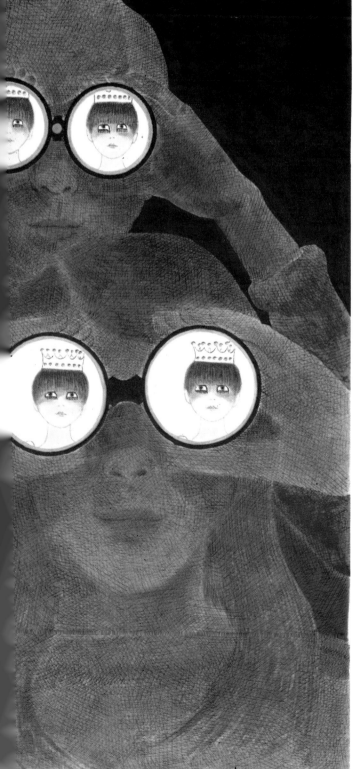

183
Book
Artist: **Tony Chen**
Art Director: **Frank Crump/Charlotte Staub**
Publisher: **L. W. Singer Co.**

184
Book
Artist: **Don Weller**
Art Director: **Gary Marshall**
Publisher: **Holloway House Publishers**

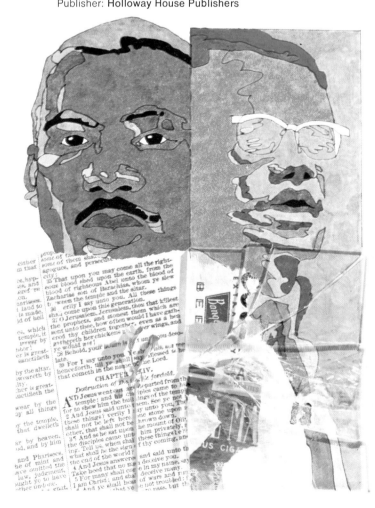

185
Advertising
Artist: Howard Rogers
Art Director: Dick Yocum
Agency: Kenyon & Eckhardt, Inc.
Client: Lincoln Mercury

186
Advertising
Artist: David Chestnutt
Art Director: David Chestnutt
Client: Richardson's Extermination

188
Institutional
Artist: **Kit Hinrichs**
Art Director: **Lou Portuesi**
Publisher: **Reader's Digest**

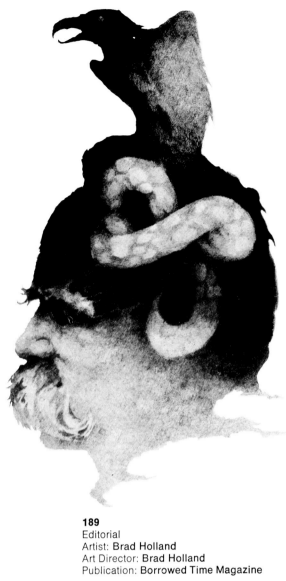

189
Editorial
Artist: **Brad Holland**
Art Director: **Brad Holland**
Publication: **Borrowed Time Magazine**

190
Advertising
Artist: **Herb Rogoff**
Art Director: **Carol Marunas**
Client: **Turn-About Records**

7
vertising
ist: Ken Dallison
Director: Jack Lardis
ency: J. Walter Thompson Co.
ent: United States Lines

191
Editorial
Artist: **Arthur Shilstone**
Art Director: **Reg Massie**
Publication: **The Reporter**

2
Institutio
Artist: **Jim Jons**
Art Director: **Henry Sanfc**
Agency: **Rowe & Sanfc**
Client: **Pan American Airlin**

201

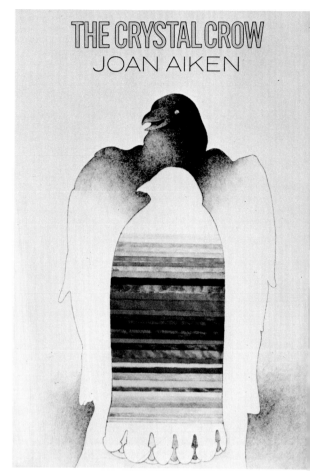

202

20

201
Book
Artist: Terence McKee
Art Director: Norman Monath
Publisher: Cornerstone Library

202
Book
Artist: James Cooper
Art Director: Margo Herr
Publisher: Doubleday & Co.

203
Book
Artist: Daniel Schwartz

204
Book
Artist: Robert Amft
Art Director: Hal Kearney
Publisher: Scott Foresman & Co.

205
Institutional
Artist: Jerry Pinkney
Art Director: Fred Andrews
Client: Manufacturers Mutual Fire
  Insurance Co.

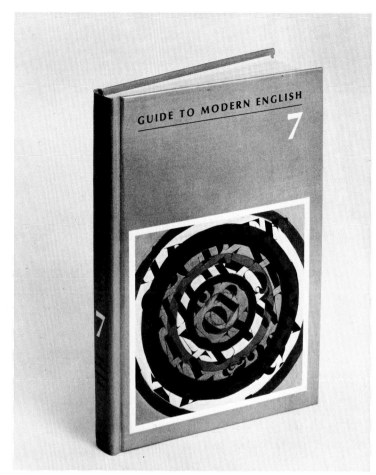

204

205

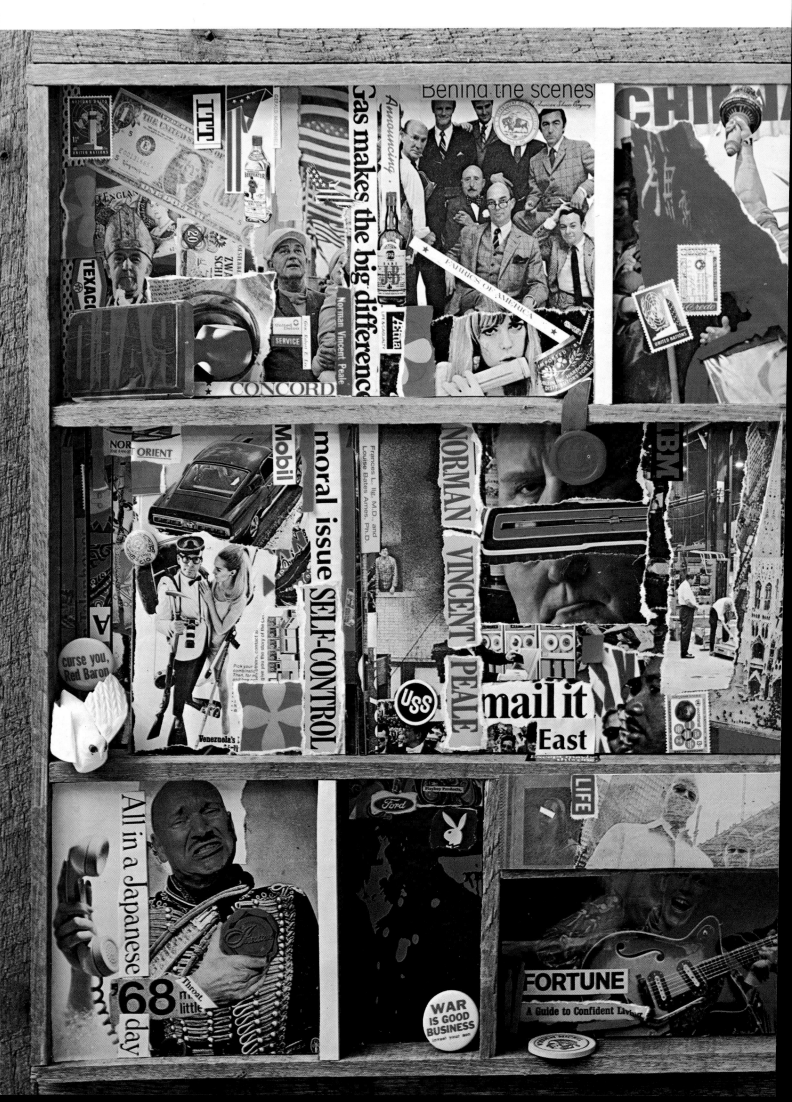

ANALYZING THE SOURCES OF LEGITIMACY
MAY HELP BRIDGE THE GAP BETWEEN
TODAY'S YOUNG PEOPLE AND BUSINESS.

THE DYNAMICS OF SOCIETY

BY KENNETH E. BOULDING

Text starts on page 4

207
Institutional
Artist: **Charles Saxon**
Art Director: **Milton Fisher**
Client: **Volkswagen of America**

Rebecca

A CONDENSATION OF
THE BOOK BY
Daphne du Maurier

ILLUSTRATED BY
DIANE AND LEO DILLON

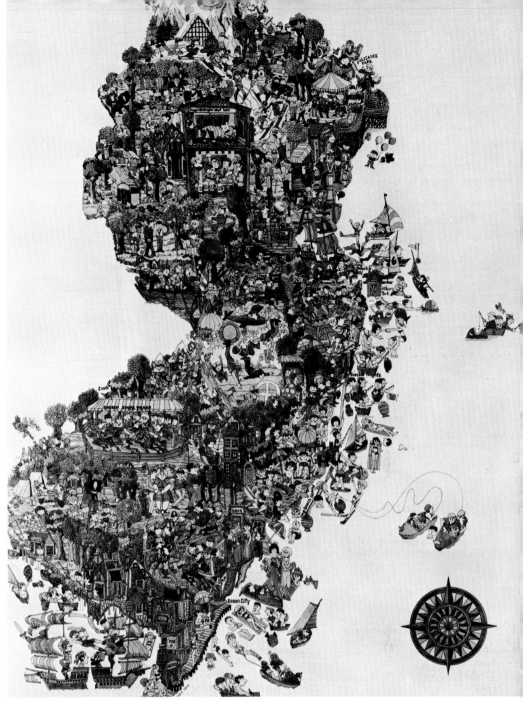

tising
David Klein
rector: Jim Flaherty
Trans World Airlines

210
Advertising
Artist: **Joseph Veno**
Art Director: **Joseph Veno**
Client: **U.S. Chamber of Commerce**

Leo and Diane Dillon
ector: Ken Hine/Don Hedin
Title: Modern Classics of Suspense
her: Reader's Digest Books

211
Book
Artist: **James Temple**

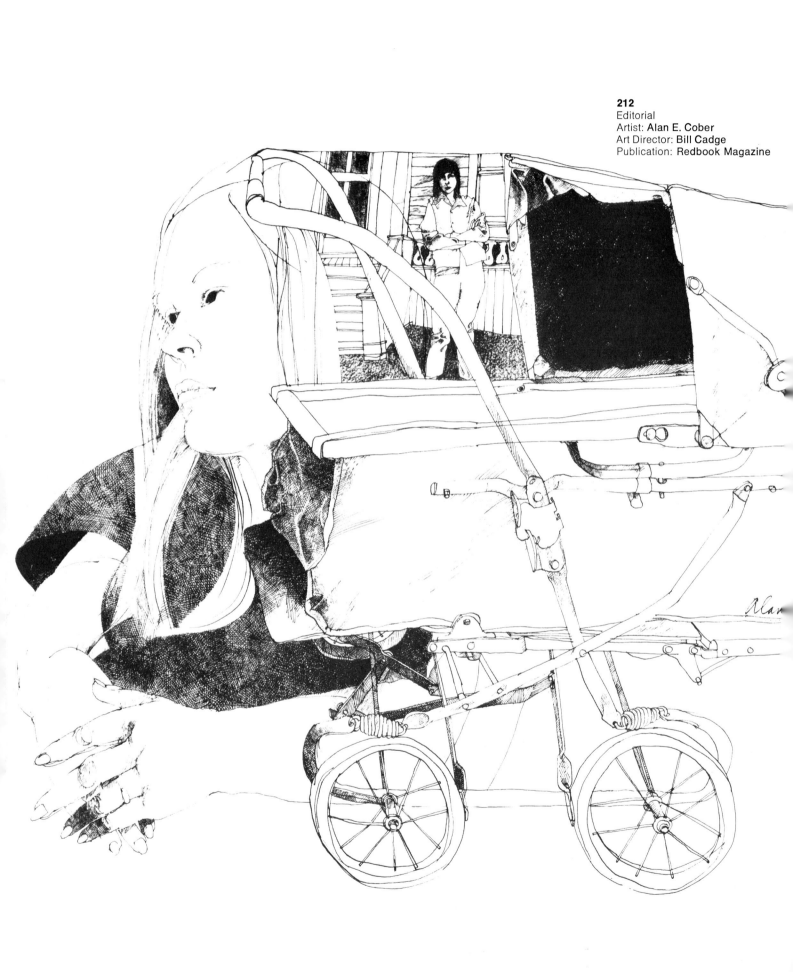

212
Editorial
Artist: **Alan E. Cober**
Art Director: **Bill Cadge**
Publication: **Redbook Magazine**

213
Editorial
Artist: Hugo Wetli
Art Director: Walter Allner
Publication: Fortune Magazine

215
Editorial
Artist: Bruce Petty
Art Director: Walter Allner
Publication: Fortune Magazine

214
Editorial
Artist: Morris Braderson
Art Director: Otto Storch/Werner Kappes
Publication: McCall's Magazine

216
Book
Artist: Charles Harper
Art Director: Ole Risom
Publisher: Western Publishing Co., Inc.

217
Book
Artist: Jim Spanfeller
Art Director: Margo Herr
Publisher: Doubleday & Co.

218
Advertising
Artist: Dave Passalacqua
Art Director: Elmer Pizzi
Agency: Gray & Rogers, Inc.
Client: United Engineers

219
Editorial
Artist: Lemuel Line
Art Director: Sam Antupit
Publication: Esquire Magazine

220
Advertising
Artist: Fred Otnes

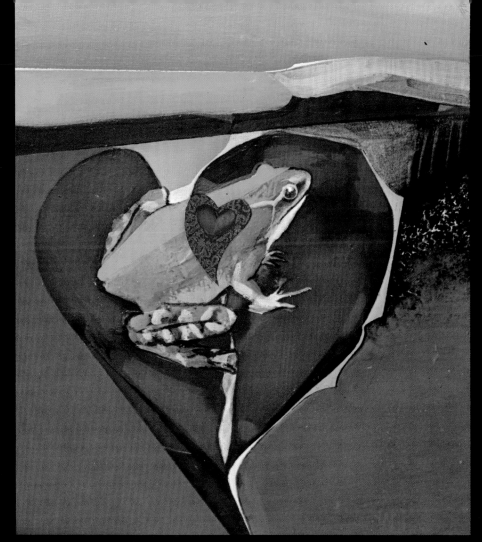

222
Institutional
Artist: Victor R. Valla
Art Director: Robert Maharry

223
Book
Artist: Nita Engle
Art Director: Ken Hine / Donald Hedin
Publisher: Reader's Digest Books

221
Institutional
Artist: Charles McVicker
Art Director: Glenn Kipp
Client: New Jersey Bell Telephone

224

225

ertising
t: Nick Gaetano
Director: Robert McDonald
ncy: Young & Rubicam, Inc.
nt: Eastern Airlines

orial
t: Nola Langner

227
Editorial
Artist: **James Cooper**
Art Director: **Jerry Smokler**
Publication: **Town & Country**

rial
Marvin Hayes
rector: Otto Storch
cation: McCall's Magazine

228
Advertising
Artist: **Ken Dallison**
Agency: **McCann Erickson Co., Toronto**
Client: **Honda**

229

230

232
Institutional
Artist: Don Weller
Art Director: Dave Boss
Client: National Football League Properties

231
Institutional
Artist: David L. Johnson
Art Director: Don Smith/Jack Robson
Agency: Ketchum, MacLeod & Grove, Inc.
Client: Scott Paper Co.

229
Editorial
Artist: Gerry Gersten
Art Director: Herb Bleiweiss/BruceDanbrot
Publication: Ladies' Home Journal

230
Advertising
Artist: Robert T. McCall
Art Director: Burt Kleeger
Agency: William Schneider Agency
Client: M.G.M.

233
Institutional
Artist: Ken Dallison
Art Director: Tom McLain
Client: B. F. Goodrich Co.

234
Institutional
Artist: **Ron Chereskin**
Art Director: **Ron Chereskin**
Client: **Dear Love Corp.**

235
Institutional
Artist: **Bob Peak**
Art Director: **Walt Reed**
Client: **Famous Artists School**

B.Peak

236

237

241

240

239

238

242

238
Advertising
Artist: Roger Hane
Art Director: John Baeder
Agency: Smith Greenland
Client: WMCA

236
Advertising
Artist: Charles Santore
Art Director: Richard Herdegan
Client: Avril Rayon

237
Institutional
Artist: R. O. Bleckman
Art Director: Louis Portuesi
Publisher: Reader's Digest

239
Editorial
Artist: David Levine
Art Director: Walter Bernard/Milton Glaser
Publication: New York Magazine

240
Editorial
Artist: James Barkley

241
Advertising
Artist: Ron Wolin
Art Director: Dave Boss
Client: N.F.L. Properties

242
Advertising
Artist: Fred Greenhill
Art Director: Martin Stevens
Client: Revlon, Inc.

243

244
Book
Artist: **Bill Greer**
Art Director: **Harald Peter**
Client: **Hallmark Cards, Inc.**

243
Institutional
Artist: **Hedda**
Art Director: **Bob Mentkin**
Agency: **J. E. McKibbon, Inc.**
Client: **Astra Pharmaceutical Products, Inc.**

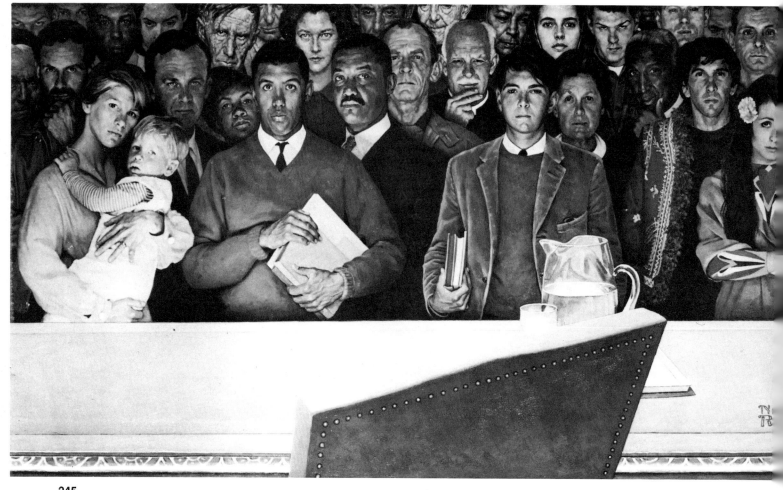

245

247

248

246
Editorial
Artist: **Norman Rockwell**
Art Director: **Allen Hurlburt**
Publication: **Look Magazine**

245
Book
Artist: **Paul Calle**

247
Book
Artist: **John Falter**
Art Director: **Ken Hine/Donald Hedin**
Publisher: **Reader's Digest Books**

248
Editorial
Artist: **Gene Szafran**
Art Director: **Arthur Paul**
Publication: **Playboy Magazine**

249
Institutional
Artist: **Jack Unruh**
Art Director: **George Buckow**
Publisher: **Houston Post**

246

249

250

251

252

253

254

255

MY SON THE MURDERER

by Bernard Malamud

Flesh of my flesh he is, bone of my bone—why can't he talk to me already?

257

258

259

260

259
Editorial
Artist: **Brad Holland**
Art Director: **Herb Lubalin**
Publication: **Avant-Garde Magazine**

260
Editorial
Artist: **Fred Otnes**
Art Director: **Bob Hallook**
Client: **Local One — Amalgamated
          Lithographers of America**
Publication: **Lithopinion**

261
Editorial
Artist: **Wilson McLean**
Art Director: **Wilson McLean**

261

262

EYE'S HOLIDAY LOVE CARDS

The usual words for Christmas cards have been overworked beyond our tolerance limits.
We prefer to send you our love in these drawings, and leave you
to find your own words to write to someone you love.
Just cut the cards from the poster and use them for gift enclosures, tie them
to a tree, or splurge madly and use the whole poster to wrap one package.

263

264

265

266
Editorial
Artist: Wilson McLean
Art Director: Denis Larkin
Agency: L. W. Frohlich / Intercon
Client: Ames Co., Division of Miles Lab.

268
Book
Artist: Seymour Leichman
Art Director: Diane Klemin
Publisher: Doubleday & Co.

269
Advertising
Artist: Ronald Searle
Art Director: Robert Colton
Agency: Ketchum, MacLeod & Grove, In
Client: Air Express

270
Book
Artist: James Barkley
Art Director: Bob Scudalari
Publisher: Pantheon Books

268

269

And so it was in each town. They came to see the boy who sang away sadness. The boy who sang pictures. And Ben did not disappoint them. The images came pouring out. Here a bull, there a dove. Emeralds and golden crowns and laughing children. All floated through the sky that spring. Roses and lilacs, and angels hung on the horizon. Sometimes he would sing just one little butterfly. Sometimes he filled the sky with them.

Once just for the fun he sang Zoomac. And Zoomac saw himself appear in the sky. In one town he sang a whole symphony orchestra and the audience not only saw them but heard them as well. That was a great deal of work and not easy to do. Mostly he sang just pictures.

His visions were never grim. Once he sang an old farmer young again. And when the old farmer saw himself young, dancing above the heat waves, he remembered better days and smiled, really smiled.

He sang of bread and wine, of milk and honey. He sang of barges on the Nile. And even the blind could see them. Such was the miracle. When he sang "the cow jumped over the moon," you can just bet it did. For an old woman whose sons were away to war, he sang them back for a while. And she saw and she felt better.

They all came and for each there was something. For Ben, too. He was no longer powerless against the sadness.

So the spring went into the summer. Word of him spread like the wind. In the smallest village, in the largest city, they knew him.

41

267
Advertising
Artist: Toni Moretto
Art Director: Rudy Sanchez / Roger Core
Agency: L. W. Frohlich & Intercon
Client: Schering Corp.

270

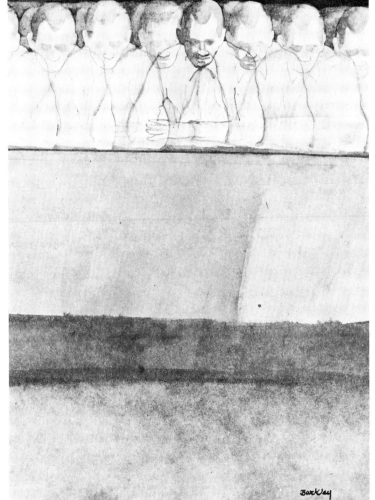

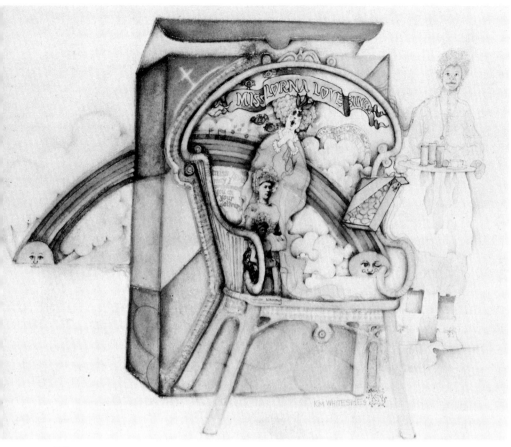

271
Editorial
Artist: Kim Whitesides
Art Director: Otto Storch / Werner Kappes
Publication: McCall's Magazine

272
Book
Artist: Robert Giusti
Art Director: Lynn Hatfield
Publisher: The Dial Press

275

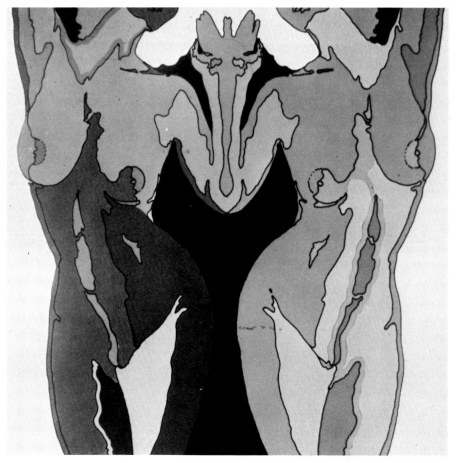

273
Book
Artist: Roger Hane
Art Director: Pat Steir
Publisher: Harper & Row

274
Editorial
Artist: Barrington Smith

275
Editorial
Artist: Isadore Seltzer

276
Institutional
Artist: David L. Johnson
Art Director: Don Smith / Jack Robson
Agency: Ketchum, MacLeod & Grove, Inc.
Client: Scott Paper Co.

273

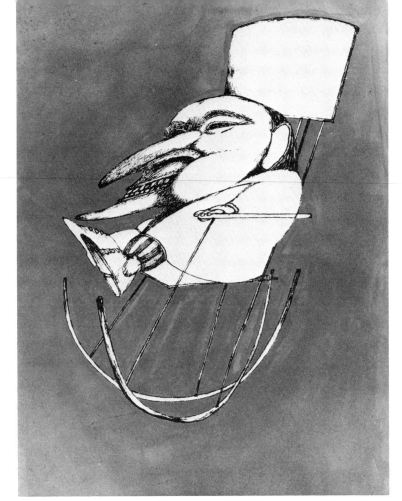

274

276

277
Book
Artist: Robert A. DeCoste
Art Director: Nancy Weare
Publisher: Ginn & Co.

278
Book
Artist: Etienne Delessert
Art Director: Etienne Delessert
Publisher: C.R.V. Lausanne, Switzerland

279
Advertising
Artist: Robert T. McCall
Art Director: Burt Kleeger
Agency: William Schneider Agency
Client: M.G.M.

280

281

282

80
ditorial
rtist: Alex Gnidziejko
rt Director: Ulrich Boege
ublisher: Status Magazine

81
ditorial
rtist: Edward Sorel
rt Director: Samuel Antupit
ublication: Esquire Magazine

82
dvertising
rtist: Leo and Diane Dillon
rt Director: Tal Stubis / John Wanek
gency: Bill Gold Advertising, Inc.
lient: Warner Bros. / Seven Arts, Inc.

283
Institutional
Artist: Donald Dubowski
Art Director: Jeannette Lee
Client: Hallmark Cards, Inc.

284
Editorial
Artist: David Chestnutt
Art Director: Paul Lynch
Client: Toronto Life

285
Institutional
Artist: Gene Holtan
Art Director: Ron Firebaugh
Client: Neiman-Marcus

283

84

285

286
Institutional
Artist: **Lionel Kalish**
Art Director: **Lionel Kalish**
Client: **Sanders Printing Co.**

288
Advertising
Artist: **Jacqui Morgan**
Art Director: **Gerry Siano**
Agency: **N. W. Ayer & Son**
Client: **DeBeers Diamonds**

287
Institutional
Artist: **James McMullan**
Art Director: **Alan Schwartzman**
Client: **The Assumptionists**

289
Book
Artist: **Tom Feelings**
Publisher: **Thomas Y. Crowell Co.**

290
Book
Artist: **Etienne Delessert**
Art Director: **Etienne Delessert/Lynn Hatfield**
Publisher: **The Dial Press**

292
Institutional
Artist: **Bernard D'Andrea**

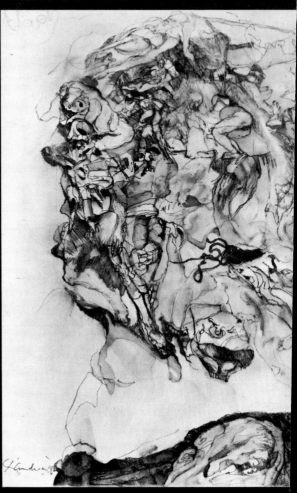

291
Editorial
Artist: **Phil Hayes**
Art Director: **Milton Glaser**
Publication: **New York Magazine**

293
Book
Artist: George Roth
Art Director: Bruce Kartebei
Publisher: Harper & Row

294
Advertising
Artist: **Jack Davis**
Art Director: **Alan Zwiebel**
Agency: **Young & Rubicam, Inc.**
Client: **Manufacturers Hanover Trust Co.**

295
Advertising
Artist: **Tony Eubanks**
Art Director: **Bob Holman**
Agency: **Wyatt, Dunagan & Williams**
Client: **Theatre Three**

296
Editorial
Artist: **James McMullan**
Art Director: **Arthur Paul**
Publication: **Playboy Magazine**

297
Editorial
Artist: Bruce Johnson
Art Director: Frank Walker
Publication: Montreal Star

298
Advertising
Artist: Milton Glaser
Art Director: Phil Parker
Agency: Wells, Rich, Greene
Client: Boodles Gin

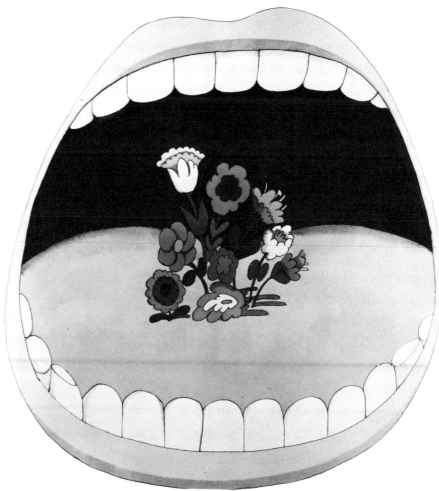

299
Editorial; Artist: **Joseph Modica**

300
Editorial; Artist: **Charles Schorre**; Art Director: **Arthur Paul**; Publication: **Playboy Magazine**

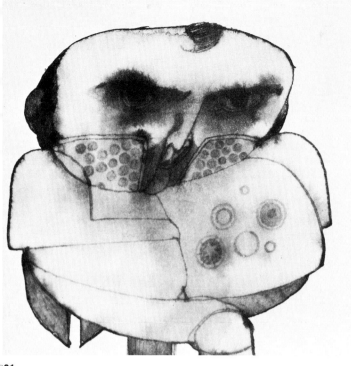

302
Book
Artist: Renate Kalkofen
Art Director: R. C. Bartlett
Publisher: D. C. Heath & Co.

301
Book
Artist: Barrington Smith

303
Editorial; Artist: **Robert Weaver**; Art Director: **Richard Gangel**; Publication: **Sports Illustrated**

304
Editorial
Artist: Gilbert L. Stone
Art Director: Neil Shakery
Agency: L. W. Frohlich & Co./Intercon
Client: Ames Co./Division Miles Laboratories

305
Editorial
Artist: David Pachman

306
Book
Artist: **James Bama**
Art Director: **Leonard Leone**
Publisher: **Bantam Books, Inc.**

307
Institutional; Artist: **Annie Chazottes**; Art Director: **Jeannette Lee**; Client: **Hallmark Cards, Inc.**

308*
Book
Artist: **Etienne Delessert**
Art Director: **Etienne Delessert/Eleonore Schmid**
Publisher: **Harlin Quist Books**

309
Editorial
Artist: **Thomas B. Allen**
Art Director: **Richard Gangel**
Publication: **Sports Illustrated**

310
Editorial
Artist: David Chestnutt
Art Director: Marg Hill
Publication: Globe & Mail

311
Editorial; Artist: Hans Falk; Art Director: Walter Allner; Publication: Fortune Magazine

312
Advertising
Artist: **Ted Coconis**
Art Director: **Bill Gold**
Agency: **Bill Gold Advertising, Inc.**
Client: **Warner Bros. — Seven Arts Inc.**

314

315

313**

313**
Book
Artist: Alan E. Cober
Art Director: Jane Bierhorst
Publisher: Hill & Wang

314
Advertising
Artist: Paul Melia
Art Director: Dan Johnson
Agency: H. H. Art Studios
Client: Baldwin Piano & Organ

315
Editorial
Artist: Harvey Gabor
Art Director: Harvey Gabor
Agency: McCann Erickson, Inc.

316
Institutional
Artist: Don Weller
Art Director: Don Weller
Client: Art Directors Club of Los Angeles

316

318
Advertising
Artist: Lorraine Fox

317
Editorial
Artist: Robert T. Handville
Client: UNICEF

320
Advertising
Artist: Joseph Veno
Art Director: Joseph Veno
Agency: Reach, McClinton
Client: Tenneco Chemical

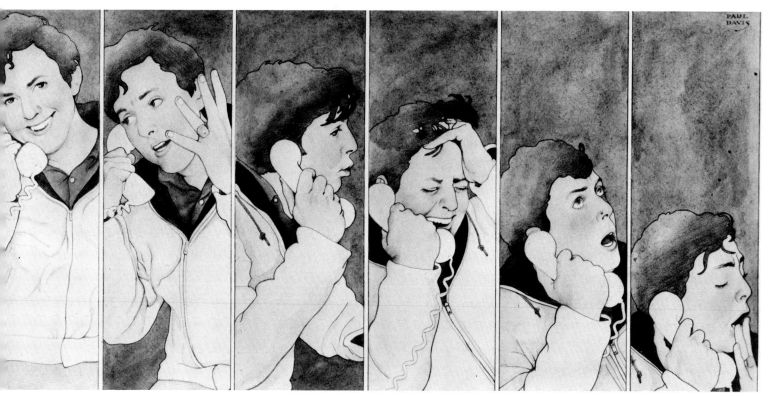

319
Editorial
Artist: Paul Davis
Art Director: Pasquale Del Vecchio
Publisher: McCall's Magazine

321
Advertising
Artist: Bob Peak
Art Director: Jules Halfant
Client: Vanguard Records

322
Editorial
Artist: Daniel Schwartz
Art Director: Alvin Grossman
Publication: Venture Magazine

411
Advertising
Artist: Don Silverstein
Art Director: David Stead
Agency: Bruce Friedlich & Co.
Client: The Curtiss-Wright Corp.

413
Book; Artist: Marti Shohet

412
Advertising
Artist: Milton Glaser
Art Director: Robert McDonald
Agency: Young & Rubicam, Inc.
Client: Eastern Airlines

414
Advertising
Artist: James Cooper
Art Director: Andy Kner
Client: Esquire Good Grooming Guide

415
Editorial
Artist: Domenico Gnoli
Art Director: Henneth Munowitz
Publication: Horizon Magazine

Note: Due to technical problems in the make-up of this book, we regret that the illustrations following No. 322 are not arranged in numerical sequence.

323*
Book
Artist: Eric VonSchmidt
Art Director: Leonard Leone
Publisher: Bantam Books, Inc.

324
Editorial
Artist: Simms Taback
Art Director: Herb Lubalin
Publication: Avant-Garde Magazine

326
Editorial
Artist: **Etienne Delessert**
Art Director: **Herb Lubalin**
Publication: **Avant-Garde Magazine**

327
Advertising
Artist: **Paul Calle**
Art Director: **Eugene Kolomatsky**
Client: **N. B. C.**

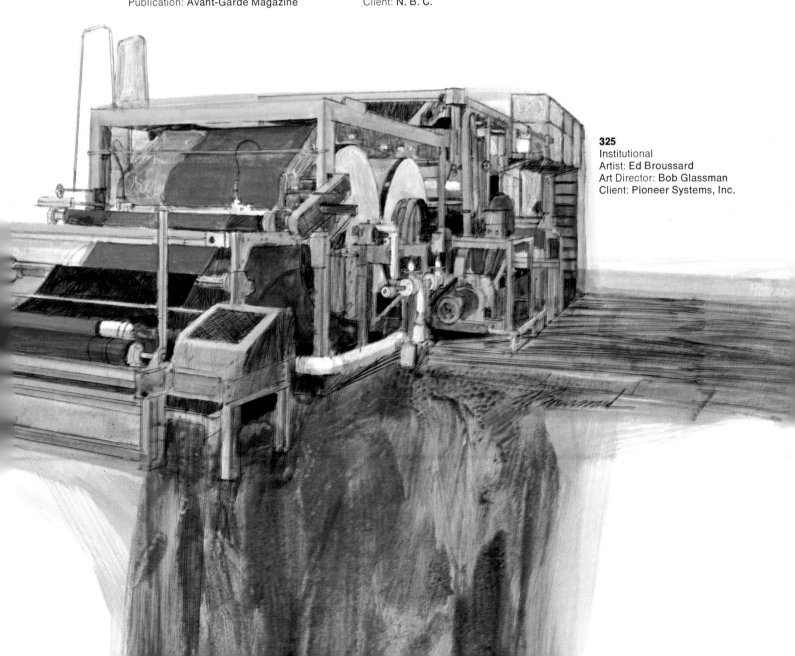

325
Institutional
Artist: **Ed Broussard**
Art Director: **Bob Glassman**
Client: **Pioneer Systems, Inc.**

417
Editorial
Artist: **John Alcorn**
Art Director: **Otto Storch/Pasquale Del Vecchio**
Publication: **McCall's Magazine**

16*
Institutional
Artist: **Paul Calle**
Art Director: **William Everhart**
Client: **National Park Service**

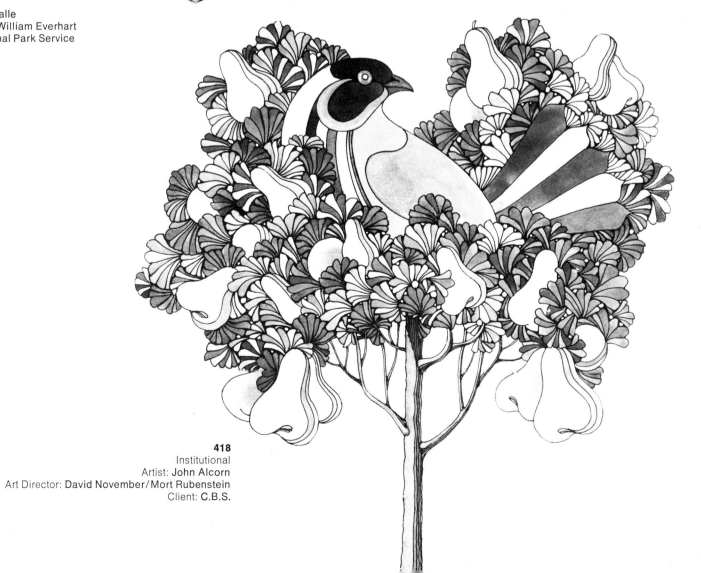

418
Institutional
Artist: **John Alcorn**
Art Director: **David November/Mort Rubenstein**
Client: **C.B.S.**

Lockheed helped man reach a new high.

And will help man work at a new low.

338

339

341

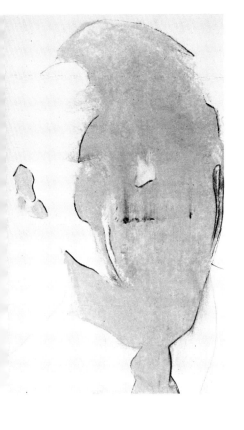

340

342

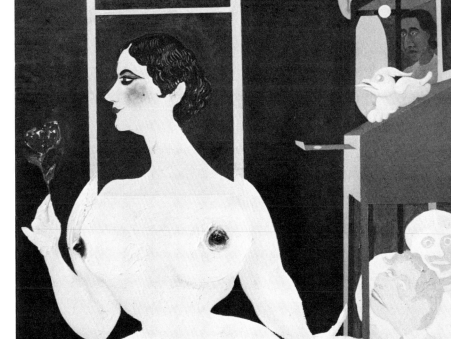

343
Advertising
Artist: Gerry Gersten
Art Director: Bob Defrin
Client: R.C.A. Victor

344
Editorial
Artist: Beni Montresor
Art Director: Otto Storch
Publication: McCall's Magazine

345
Book
Artist: Tom Lovell
Art Director: Andrew Poggenpohl
Publisher: National Geographic Society

419

422

423

419
Advertising
Artist: Murray Tinkelman

420
Book
Artist: Gene Szafran
Art Director: Connie Avon
Publisher: Benziger Bros., Inc.

421
Editorial
Artist: Edward Sorel
Art Director: Samuel Antupit
Publisher: Esquire Magazine

422
Institutional
Artist: Don Weller
Art Director: Dave Boss
Client: National Football League

423
Editorial
Artist: Stephen Antonakos
Art Director: Herb Lubalin
Publication: Avant-Garde Magazine

421

20

332
Book
Artist: Jack White
Art Director: Suzanne Snider/Hal Kearney
Publisher: Scott Foresman & Co.

334
Institutional
Artist: Robert T. Handville
Client: Artists Associates

333
Book
Artist: Eleonore Schmid
Art Director: Eleonore Schmid
Publisher: Annette Betz Verlag,
Munich, Germany

335
Editorial
Artist: Wilson McLean
Art Director: Don Menell
Publication: Cavalier Magazine

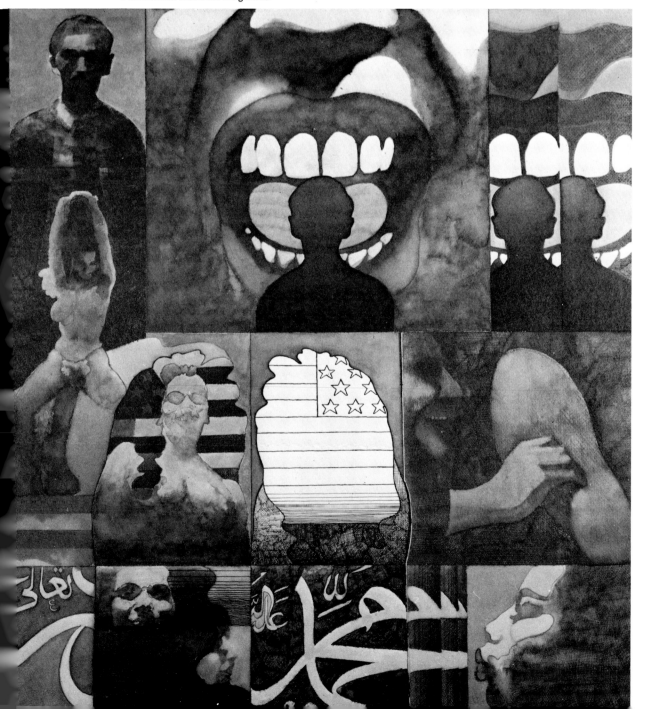

424

425

424
Editorial
Artist: Gordon Kibbee
Art Director: Arthur Paul
Publication: Playboy Magazine

425
Institutional
Artist: Milton Charles
Art Director: Sol Immerman
Client: Washington Square Press

426
Advertising
Artist: William Hofmann
Art Director: Bil Harvey
Client: Electra Records

Edit
Artist: Daniel M
Art Director: Andrew
Publication: Print Maga

426

336
Book
Artist: **William Hofmann**
Art Director: **Leonard Leone**
Publisher: **Bantam Books, Inc.**

337
Advertising
Artist: **Charles Bragg**
Art Director: **John Berg**
Client: **Columbia Records**

The Ark
Chad Stuart
& Jeremy Clyde

428

428
Editorial
Artist: Beni Montresor
Art Director: Otto Storch/Werner Kappes
Publication: McCall's Magazine

429

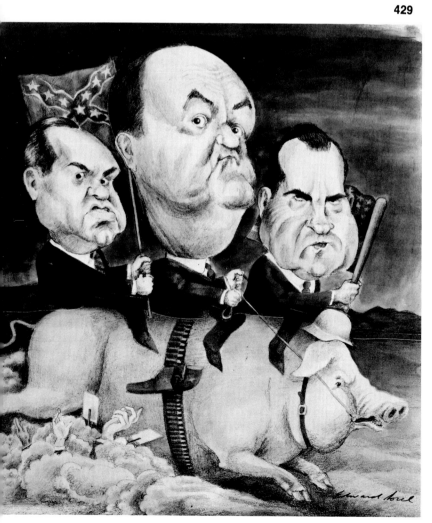

429
Editorial
Artist: Edward Sorel
Art Director: Kenneth Deardoff
Publication: Evergreen Review

430
Book
Artist: Paul Williams

346
Book
Artist: **Charles Mikolaycak**
Art Director: **Morris Kerchoff**
Publisher: **Allyn & Bacon, Inc.**

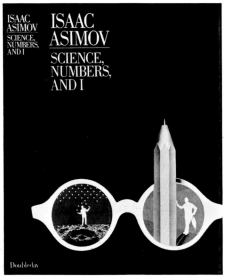

347
Book
Artist: **Peter Rauch**
Art Director: **Margo Herr**
Publisher: **Doubleday & Co.**

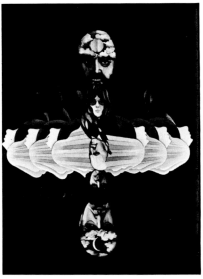

348
Editorial
Artist: **Charles White III**
Art Director: **Samuel Antupit**
Publisher: **Esquire Magazine**

349
Institutional
Artist: Alan E. Cober
Art Director: Dean Powell
Agency: Young & Rubicam, Inc.
Client: Artists Guild of N.Y.C.

350
Book
Artist: Shannon Stirnweis
Art Director: Bob Blanchard
Publisher: Ballantine Books

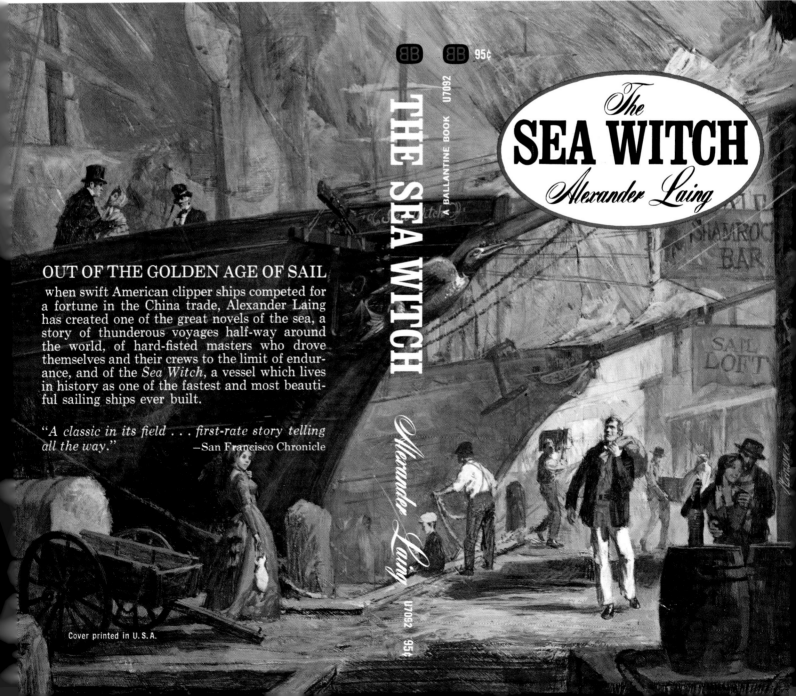

95¢

U7092

A BALLANTINE BOOK

THE SEA WITCH

Alexander Laing

The
SEA WITCH
Alexander Laing

SHAMROCK BAR

SAIL LOFT

OUT OF THE GOLDEN AGE OF SAIL

when swift American clipper ships competed for
a fortune in the China trade, Alexander Laing
has created one of the great novels of the sea, a
story of thunderous voyages half-way around
the world, of hard-fisted masters who drove
themselves and their crews to the limit of endur-
ance, and of the *Sea Witch*, a vessel which lives
in history as one of the fastest and most beautiful sailing ships ever built.

*"A classic in its field . . . first-rate story telling
all the way."*
—San Francisco Chronicle

Cover printed in U.S.A.

U7092 95¢

431
Advertising
Artist: Robert Weaver
Art Director: Windsor Mallett/Gordon Hammond
Publisher: Christian Science Monitor
Agency: B.B.D.O., Boston

432
Book
Artist: Betty Fraser
Art Director: Diane Klemin
Publisher: Doubleday & Co.

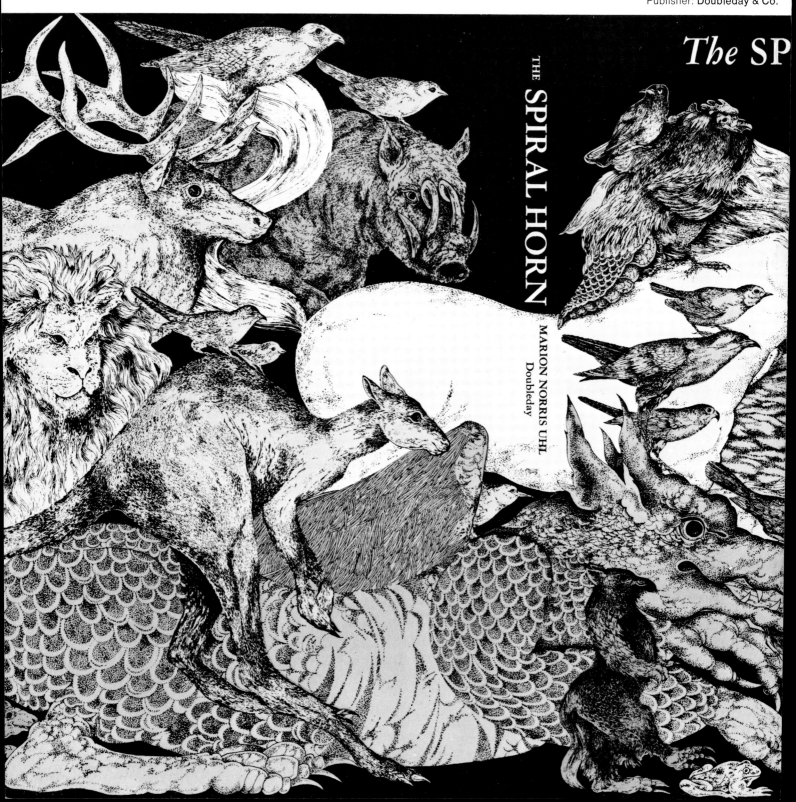

433
Advertising
Artist: John Janus
Art Director: Tom Clemente
Agency: Bureau of Advertising
Client: Member Newspapers

L HORN

N NORRIS UHL

trated by Betty Fraser

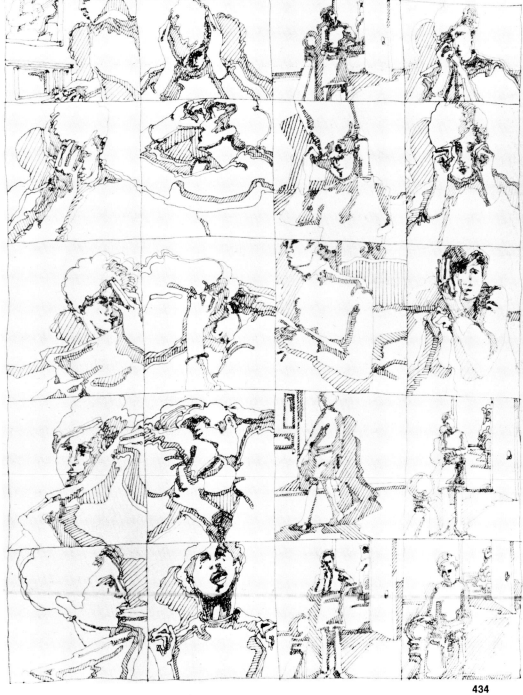

434
Editorial
Artist: Donna Brown
Art Director: Joan Fenton
Publication: Seventeen Magazine

353
Editorial
Artist: Teresa Fasolino

354
Advertising
Artist: Barron Storey
Art Director: Bill Foster
Agency: B.B.D.O., Inc.
Client: General Electric Co.

371
Book
Artist: H. D. Stallworth
Art Director: Muriel Underwood
Publisher: Follett Publishing Co.

torial
t: Jim Spanfeller
Director: Arthur Paul
lication: Playboy Magazine

366
Institutional
Artist: Linda Kaye Recker
Art Director: Louis Mainieri
Client: Kohler & Sons Printing

351
Editorial
Artist: **Howard Sanden**
Art Director: **Kenneth Stuart**
Publication: **Reader's Digest**

352
Institutional
Artist: **Murray Tinkelman**
Art Director: **Murray Tinkelman**
Client: **Artists Associates**

359
Book
Artist: Norman Laliberte'
Art Director: Morris Kirchoff
Publisher: Allyn & Bacon, Inc.

360
Institutional
Artist: Jean Leon Huens
Art Director: Ken Sneider/Murray Miller
Publisher: Reader's Digest

362
Institutional
Artist: **Robert Aulicino**
Art Director: **Margo Herr**
Publisher: **Doubleday & Co.**

363
Advertising
Artist: **Ronald Stein**
Art Director: **Jerry Siano**
Agency: **N. W. Ayer & Son, Inc.**
Client: **DeBeers/Kimberley Union of South Africa**

364
Advertising
Artist: **Abe Gurvin**
Art Director: **Bill Harvey**
Client: **Nonesuch Records**

ertising
st: **Reynold Ruffins**
Director: **Stanley White**
it: **Lutheran Church of America**

390
Book
Artist: **Sanford Kossin**
Art Director: **George Paturzo**
Publisher: **Berkeley Books**

391
Book
Artist: **Anthony Saris**
Art Director: **Allen Carr**
Publisher: **Follett Publishing Co.**

Lingonberries in the Snow

Britta-Lisa Joutsen

·TAX SHELTER·

368
Institutional
Artist: Donald M. Hedin

367
Editorial
Artist: Don Weller
Art Director: Mike Salisbury
Publication: West Magazine

369
Advertising
Artist: John Gundelfinger
Art Director: Frank Gauna
Client: United Artists Records

370*
Book
Artist: Eleonore Schmid
Art Director: Eleonore Schmid
Publisher: Harlin Quist Books

397
Advertising
Artist: Dave Passalacqua
Art Director: Elmer Pizzi
Agency: Gray & Rogers, Inc.
Client: United Engineers

398
Book
Artist: Leo and Diane Dillon
Art Director: Louise Noble
Publisher: Houghton Mifflin Co.

373
Advertising
Artist: **Howard Terpning**
Art Director: **Robert Blend**
Agency: **Griswold-Eshleman**
Client: **General Cigar Co.**

374
Advertising
Artist: **Frank Bozzo**
Art Director: **William Harvey**
Client: **Nonesuch Records**

375
Book
Artist: **Eugene Pawlowski**
Art Director: **Bert Benkendorf**
Agency: **Edward Howard Co.**
Client: **California Institute Technology**

376
Book
Artist: **Richard Cuffari**
Art Director: **Bill Gregory**
Publisher: **New American Library**

373

377
Advertising
Artist: **Milton Glaser**
Art Director: **Phil Parker**
Agency: **Wells, Rich & Greene**
Client: **Boodles Gin**

404
Book
Artist: **Tony Chen**
Art Director: **Frank Crump**
Publisher: **L. W. Singer Co.**

405
Book
Artist: **John Falter**
Art Director: **Ken Hine/Donald Hedin**
Publisher: **Reader's Digest Books**

406
Advertising
Artist: **Margaret Pelletieri**
Art Director: **John Berg**
Client: **Columbia Records**

378
Advertising
Artist: Robert Lockhart
Art Director: George Osaki
Client: Capitol Records

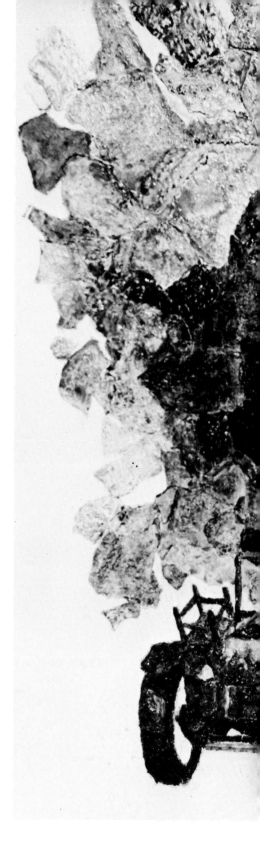

379
Institutional
Artist: Jack Unruh
Art Director: Robert Lawton
Client: Norsworthy Mercer

380
Book
Artist: David Graves

381
Book
Artist: Robert Shore
Art Director: Dave Glixon
Publisher: Limited Editions Club

382
Book
Artist: **Hans Jorgen Toming**
Art Director: **Gerald Lynas**
Publisher: **Lion Press**

383*
Institutional
Artist: **Robert A. Heindel**
Art Director: **Gery Colby**
Agency: **James Dunn & Assoc.**
Client: **Detroit Red Wings**

384
Advertising
Artist: **Paul Calle**
Art Director: **Eugen Kolomatsky**
Client: **N.B.C.**

Some young people smoke,
    others drink.
  Some even turn to drugs.
          Why?
What facts do I know about smoking...
        about drinking...
          about the use of drugs?
The crowd, the group do things just for kicks.
        Kicks are for fun,
    for feeling alive,
        for feeling free.
      Kicks are fleeting;
  Here today, gone tomorrow.
        The fun, the feeling
  of freedom fade away.
      Kicks are getting harder to find.
        Are kicks for me?

              To get out of myself...
                to escape...
              to be adult...
            to be "in" with the cro
            Just to be free!
        Every person has a right
            to freedom
    and hopes to attain it.
          Sometimes, though,
  there is a certain amount of confus
        Not everyone understands
    personal freedom and liberty
        in the same way.
          What exactly do I mean
    when I say I am free?
        St. Paul tells us
  that we are called to liberty.
        He tells us how we should
      make use of this freedom.

"My brothers, you were called, as you know,
to liberty; but be careful, or this liberty
will provide an opening for self-indulgence.
Serve one another, rather, in works of love,
since the whole of the Law is summarized
in a single command:
Love your neighbor as yourself.
If you go on snapping at each other
and tearing each other to pieces,
you had better watch or you will
destroy the whole community."
                (Galatians 5:13-15)

7-2

G.P.   68

386

387

385
Editorial
Artist: Russ Lawson

386
Editorial
Artist: Gabriel Pascalini
Art Director: Samuel Antupit
Publication: Esquire Magazine

387
Advertising
Artist: Marvin Friedman
Art Director: John Graham
Client: N.B.C.

388
Book
Artist: Richard Cuffari
Art Director: Sid Rosenberg
Publisher: Perspective Design, Inc.

389
Editorial
Artist: Edward Sorel
Art Director: Samuel Antupit
Publication: Esquire Magazine

389

392

392
Book
Artist: Leo and Diane Dillon
Art Director: Leonard Leone
Publisher: Bantam Books, Inc.

393
Editorial
Artist: Brad Holland
Art Director: William Cadge
Publication: Redbook Magazine

394
Editorial
Artist: James Hill
Art Director: Otto Storch/Pasquale Del Vecchio
Publication: McCall's Magazine

395
Institutional
Artist: Phillip H. Hays
Art Director: Richard Wachter
Agency: L. W. Frohlich & Co./Intercon
Client: CIBA

396
Institutional
Artist: Paul Giovanopoulos
Art Director: Harald Peter
Client: Hallmark Cards, Inc.

394

393

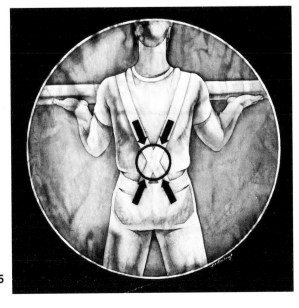

395

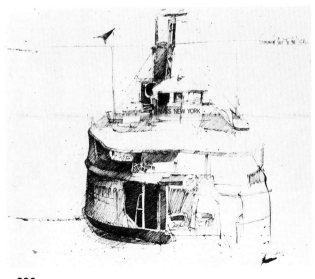

396

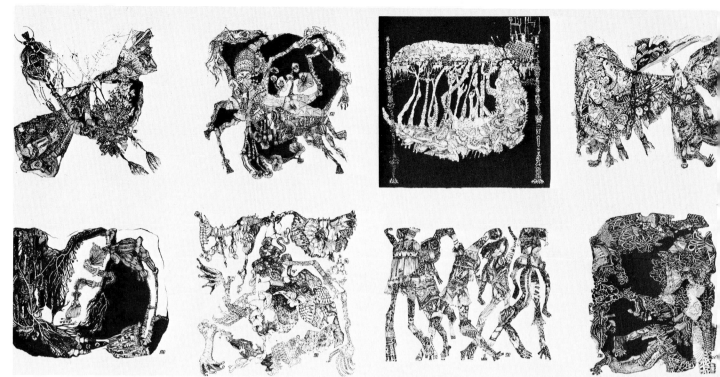

399
Book
Artist: Wolfgang Walther
Art Director: Wolfgang Walther
Publisher: Weiss-Staufacher

401

402

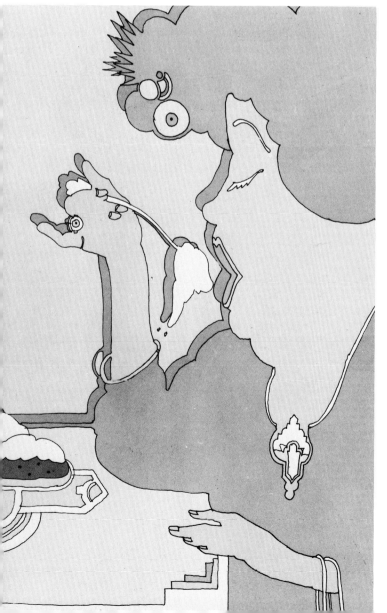

400
Institutional
Artist: George Gaadt

401
Book
Artist: Seymour Chwast
Publisher: Push Pin Graphic

402
Institutional
Artist: Donald M. Hedin

403
Artist: Stan Hunter
Art Director: Russ D'Anna
Publisher: Scholastic Books

400

403

407
Advertising
Artist: Gerry Gersten
Art Director: Paul Fromm
Agency: Young & Rubicam, Inc.
Client: Travelers Insurance Co.

409
Editorial
Artist: Gilbert L. Stone
Art Director: Richard Gangel
Publication: Sports Illustrated

408
Advertising
Artist: Marvin Friedman
Art Director: John Graham
Client: N.B.C.

410
Institutional
Artist: Bart Forbes
Art Director: Jack Reed
Agency: Wyatt, Dunagan & Williams
Client: Southfield Life Insurance

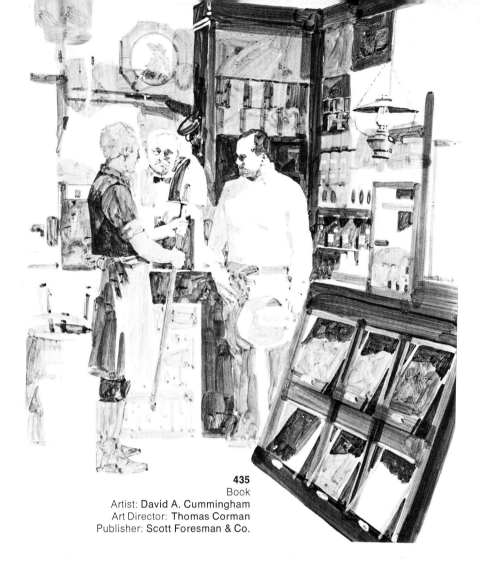

435
Book
Artist: David A. Cummingham
Art Director: Thomas Corman
Publisher: Scott Foresman & Co.

436
Editorial
Artist: Hank Virgona
Art Director: Walter Allner
Publication: Fortune Magazine

437
Institutional
Artist: Robert Brickhouse

438
Book; Artist: Murray Tinkelman

439
Editorial
Artist: **Tom Lovell**
Art Director: **Andrew Poggenpohl**
Publication: **National Geographic Society**

440
Book
Artist: **Etienne Delessert**
Publisher: **W. W. Norton & Co.**

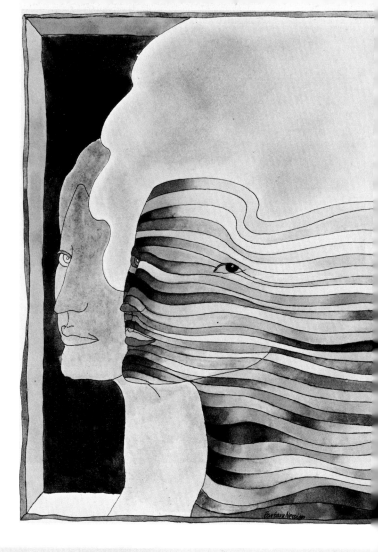

442

443

441
Editorial
Artist: Barbara Nessim
Art Director: Ulrich Boege
Publication: Status Magazine

442
Book
Artist: Alex Gotfryd
Art Director: Alex Gotfryd
Publisher: Doubleday & Co., Inc.

443
Book
Artist: Paul Giovanopoulos
Art Director: James Davis
Publisher: McGraw Hill Jr. Books

41

328
Editorial
Artist: **Bernard D'Andrea**
Art Director: **Joan Fenton**
Publication: **Seventeen Magazine**

329
Institutional
Artist: **Bernard D'Andrea**

330
Editorial
Artist: **Homer Hill (Deceased)**
Art Director: **Robert Hallock**
Publication: **Lithopinion**

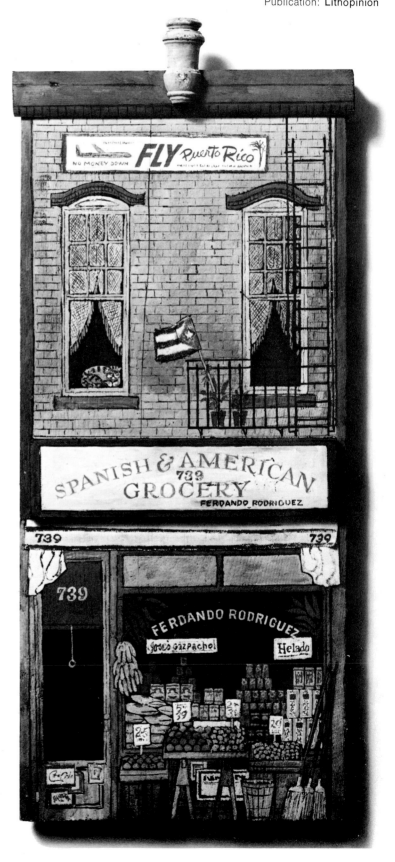

356
Institutional
Artist: Paula Powers Coe
Art Director: Maurice Yanez
Agency: Robert Miles Runyan & Assoc.
Client: American Export Isbrandtsen Lines

357
Advertising
Artist: Wilson McLean
Art Director: Jack Anish
Agency: William Schneider Agency
Client: M.G.M.

358**
Editorial
Artist: James Barkley

THE AWARD WINNERS SPEAK

Mark English

Gilbert L. Stone

Alan E. Cober

In the last Illustrator's Show I had the honor of receiving a special award, and this year the Artist's Guild of New York named me "Artist of the Year" and honored me with a dinner at the Society of Illustrators. To be singled out in this manner and placed in a small company of artists similarly honored for other years, gave me great personal satisfaction. It also called for some soul searching, and this contemplation brought certain misgivings.

My first professional job in graphics was that of an art director in a large advertising agency, and I later chose to be an illustrator. In any context the word "Illustrator" is a loose and ambiguous term. At one time or another it surely had a more precise connotation than it does today. Homer was an illustrator as was Daumier and Lautrec, giving breadth and universality to their subject matter. At later times during the "great" days of the Saturday Evening Post, a whole school of illustrators were developed. They showed us what things, places, or a group of characters looked like at a particular moment of a particular story. Their job became less important as good photographers emerged and grew, and as the movies and television come forth with staggering images. Now the "Post" illustrator hardly exists or, at least, his job hardly exists. I can not mourn this fact. To the contrary I think it is surely a burden off the illustrator today, and the results of his new independence show. Graphics in all forms have flourished.

All is not well, the illustrator is functioning like a broken field runner, winding through fads and client fancy with tricks and technique and seldom a chance to do his best or even to be himself. Still there is good graphics being done. Illustration is better than before, sometimes it's beautiful.

At a time when "Madge the manicurist" and "Josephine the plumber" are insulting the intelligence of morons; when capable art directors and designers are compromising on another photograph that will be lost in the great maze of advertising; there is a good tool of communication being almost ignored. It's not a new and improved pancea with enzymes added to work magic, but for certain problems it has merit. It is personal and unique. It can be warm and emotional. Illustration can communicate.

MARK ENGLISH

THE AGE OF PERSONAL UNIQUENESS

Today the problems of communication in mass media parallel the problems of esthetic values dealt with by painters of the Renaissance four hundred years ago. Both are involved with a personal uniqueness and a never ending task of the artists struggle with his benefactors. The patrons have changed and so has the subject matter.

The so-called barriers of fine art have been stripped away by its own intellectualism leaving only at best thin fragments of painting with long, ambiguous well written interpretations by critics and artists alike of what has been done. The 'fine artist', with exceptions, has in the past ten years made the mistake of turning to commercialism as their prime source of subject matter. I am often amazed when I hear statements from artists such as 'I discovered Norman Rockwell, what a gas!' and 'did you ever paint an apple to look real? wow!', etc. Today, the painter in his own way is attempting to do what Mr. Rockwell does so beautifully and did some thirty or forty years ago. On both scores whether it be labeled painting or illustration after function or functionlessness, what you see and call the painting is what remains for the world as proof.

In my early pictures I became concerned with a vocabulary of total organic unity. For me the challenge of surface was the most crucial point, where an object is not merely rendered real but evolves and becomes real with each phase of the painting.

The field of illustration has become what it is today as a result of the efforts of artists like Milton Glaser, Philip Hays, Robert Weaver and others, who through their personal uniqueness have made commercial art a prestigious profession.

Elaine Sorel, who as my agent, has been a constant source of guidance and inspiration to me and the artists she represents. We are at a time in illustration where people like her who pave the way with their inventiveness and sincerity help artists to produce the work we see today, with the goal to achieve nothing less than greatness.

GILBERT STONE

"STUDENTS, READ THIS MESSAGE!!"

When asked what I do for a living, I say I am a drawer. What do I draw? Pictures! What kind of pictures? Anything interesting or challenging or not so interesting and a few that are boring. "Oh," they say "for whom?" For myself, for magazines and myself, galleries and myself, books and myself, museum shows, advertising, posters, etc. I am a drawer!! They say "Oh, you mean you are a commercial artist." My answer is no, because I'm only that when I collect my checks from the mailbox, as Picasso. At all other times I am just an artist.

Since when is being paid for interpreting and executing a picture uniquely and personally with expression, feeling and craft, called commercial.
The dictionary defines —

Commercial — adj.; prepared merely for sale. I do not think I prepare anything just for sale nor do most of my cohorts.

Fine Arts — those arts which seek expression through beautiful or significant modes. I think that fits today's best illustrator-artist. More and more fit this category and more and more schools are bringing the student back to the fundamentals, where he is taught the most important elements are thinking, drawing, design and color (each of these is individually important at some stage of every picture) where he will find the very most important elements are opening your eyes to see and opening your ears to listen.

Many of you commercial artists should return to school. Photography did not put you out of business — you did, when you closed your eyes and opened your lens and shutter speeds.

ALAN E. COBER

SCHOLARSHIP COMPETITION

Of the many educational and philanthropic projects of the Society of Illustrators, one of the most successful is the Annual Scholarship Competition.

Drawing entries from colleges and professional schools across the nation, the Society calls upon juries of experienced art directors and illustrators to judge them. Selecting those to be hung in an exhibit in the Society Gallery, the judges award prizes to those of distinctive merit. The prizes are contributed by the industry to promote and stimulate new talent within the field of illustration.

This year's committee, headed by Celeste Whitney, received more than five hundred and fifty entries. The quality of the entries extraordinary revealing the presence of much fresh talent in our educational institutions. One hundred and two pieces were hung in our new gallery for the awards luncheon held in the Spring.

The Society is much indebted to all the donors, the Readers' Digest, Boy's Life, M. Grumbacher, Inc. and the Famous Artists School for their financial support.

The Mural Painters
Warwick, N.Y.

WARWICK

About fifteen years ago the "Warwick Art Project" was started by the membership of the Society of Illustrators as a public service. Since its induction every man who has been chairman has been more or less dedicated.

The Warwick project or the "Theodore (Teddy) Croslin Art Project" as it is now known consist of boys. Not just ordinary boys, but boys who have been incarcerated — who have been arrested for a crime that they have been found guilty or for some other reason have been put into what is commonly known as a reformatory, but officially is called a "State School".

These boys come from all walks of life — their ages run from ten years to sixteen years. A few come from environments where they have had all the advantages or the better things in life, but most come from disadvantage areas or slums — "black and white slums". Not just New York City, but the entire state of New York.

These kids who attend the classes look forward to seeing us, the members of our "Society" on Saturdays. It is as Mr. A. Albert Cohen the superintendent of the school has said — "It is the first time in the lives of many of these boys that they have come in contact with someone who is important, someone who is accomplished, someone who cares enough to give a little of his time to show these boys that there is something else in life besides the sordidness of crime that they have been accustomed to seeing.

The new boys in the classes are usually skeptical. It is hard for them to believe that you are there to try and give them something without looking for something in return. I have had a few ask me how much am I getting for coming up to Warwick on Saturdays.

Most of the boys who attend the classes have an honest desire to draw. Some have a great deal of ability or the potential. A few come to get away from some chore he may have to perform back at the cottage, or he may be just curious.

But at Warwick these boys are away from the home or neighborhood environs, the things in the street that influenced him and were the causes for him being at Warwick. There may be a Rembrandt, a Bernie Fuchs or a Joe Kidd, and if so he has a chance. Being a juvenile in New York the law permits him to start out with a clean slate when he's twenty one.

DAVID (DAVE) HODGES
Chairman "Theodore (Teddy) Croslin
Art Project"

BLUE CURTAIN

LLUSTRATORS

INDEX

ILLUSTRATORS

While every effort has been made to insure the accuracy of the credits in this volume, it is inevitable that an occasional error may have crept in. On behalf of the Society of Illustrators, the publishers would appreciate information about any omissions or corrections.

Note: Due to technical problems in the make-up of this book, we regret that the illustrations following No. 322 are not arranged in numerical sequence.

Fujikawa, Gyo, 53
325 East 57 Street
New York City

Gaadt, George, 252, 400
14 Wood Street
Pittsburgh, Pa.

Gabor, Harvey, 315
485 Lexington Avenue
New York City

Gaetano, Nick, 224
New York City

Gersten, Gerry, 48, 73, 229,
343, 407
51 Mallard Rise
Irvington-on-Hudson, N. Y.

Giovanopoulos, Paul, 396, 443
73 Vermilyea Ave.
New York City

Giusti, Robert, 272
350 East 52 Street
New York City

Glanzman, Lou, 341
154 Handsome Avenue
Sayville, N. Y.

Glaser, Milton, 59, 125, 178,
298, 377, 412
51 West 52 Street
New York City

Gnidziejko, Alex, 49, 145, 280
c/o Leo Wolff
20 East 9 Street
New York City

Gnoli, Domenico, 25, 415
c/o Ed Riley
252 East 49 Street
New York City

Gorey, Edward, 26
36 East 38 Street
New York Ctiy

Gotfryd, Alex, 442
Doubleday & Co., Inc.
277 Park Avenue
New York City

Graves, David, 380
1801 West 4 Street
Lawrence, Kansas

Greenhill, Fred, 242
80 East End Avenue
New York City

Greer, Bill, 58, 244
Mill River Road
South Salem, N. Y.

Gundelfinger, John, 369
152 East 22 Street
New York Ctiy

Gurvin, Abe, 364
32 East 35 Street
New York City

Hampton, Blake, 169
North Avenue
Weston, Conn.

Handville, Robert T., 317, 334
99 Woodland Drive
Pleasantville, N. Y.

Hane, Roger, 238, 273
131 East 93 Street
New York City

Harper, Charles, 216
c/o Western Publishing Co., Inc.
Golden Press Division
850 Third Avenue
New York City

Hayes, Marvin, 124, 226
58 Oregon Avenue
Bronxville, N. Y.

Hayes, Phil, 291
53 East Main Street
Huntington, N. Y.

Hays, Phillip H., 395
327 Central Park West
New York City

Hedda, 74, 243
108 West 14 Street
New York City

Hedin, Donald M., 100, 155,
368, 402
82 Westford Drive
Southport, Conn.

Heindel, Robert A., 115, 383
24855 Thorndyke
Southfield, Mich.

Helmrich, Jerry, 126

Hess, Richard, 141
155 East 50 Street
New York City

Hill, Homer, 88, 330
(deceased)

Hill, James, 1, 166, 172, 394
c/o Estelle Mandel Co., Inc.
65 East 80 Street
New York City

Hinrichs, Kit, 41, 188
150 East 35 Street
New York Ctiy

Hofmann, William, 118, 336, 426
4 Mile Point
Athens, N. Y.

Holland, Brad, 87, 189, 259, 393
639 East 11 Street
New York City

Holtan, Gene, 285

Howlett, Margaret, 92, 255
119 Haddon Place
Upper Montclair, N. J.

Huehnergarth, John, 60
33 Red Rose Way
Levittown, Pa.

Huens, Jean Leon, 360
Revers Du Grand Pre Mogorail
Pesche-Les-Couvin,
BELGIUM

Hunter, Stan, 152, 403
8301 Silvery Lane
Dearborn Heights, Mich.

Isom, Joe, 62, 63, 105
7102 West 67 Street
Shawnee Mission, Kans.

Janus, John, 433
Monogram Associates
1150 Avenue of the Americas
New York City

Jasmin, Paul, 135
c/o Esquire
488 Madison Avenue
New York City

Jebavy, James, 40, 101
c/o Higgins, Hegner, Genovese
251 East Grand
Chicago, Ill.

Johnson, Bruce, 297
Franklin Centre
Quebec, Canada

Johnson, David, 42, 231, 276
1726 Grand Avenue
San Rafael, Calif.

Johnson, Doug, 51
108 West 14 Street
New York City

Jonson, Jim, 200
125 East 83 Street
New York City

Kalish, Lionel, 16, 116, 286
105 West 55 Street
New York City

Kalkofen, Renate, 302
287 Huren Avenue
Cambridge, Mass.

Keats, Ezra Jack, 153
444 East 82 Street
New York City

Keely, John, 258
400 Clifton Avenue
Minneapolis, Minn.

Kibbee, Gordon, 81, 424
1801 Delancey Place
Philadelphia, Pa.

Klein, David, 208
281A Henry Street
Brooklyn, N. Y.

Kollar, Earnie, 264
Long Beach, Calif.

Kossin, Sanford, 390
145 East 49 Street
New York City

Lalibertè, Norman, 359
Turkhill Road
Brewster, N. Y.

Langner, Nola, 225
271 Central Park West
New York City

Lawson, Russ, 385
327 East 13 Street
New York City

Leichman, Seymour, 268
276 Riverside Drive
New York City

Levine, David, 239
58 Montgomery Place
Brooklyn, N. Y.

Lewin, Ted, 173
21 Saint James Place
Brooklyn, N. Y.

Line, Lemuel, 219
1424 Flat Rock Road
Narberth, Pa.

Lobel, Arnold, 149
618A Third Street
Brooklyn, N. Y.

Lockhart, Robert, 103, 150, 378
1750 North Vine Street
Los Angeles, Calif.

Lovell, Tom, 45, 162, 345, 439
3 Skytop Drive
East Norwalk, Conn.

Lubalin, Herb, Inc., 19
223 East 31 Street
New York City

Lund, Gary, 14
1520 North Sierra Bonita
Los Angeles, Calif.

Maffia, Daniel, 154, 427
200 East 95 Street
New York City

Mandel, John, 339
New York Ctiy

Mattelson, Marvin, 85
2006 Glenview Street
Philadelphia, Pa.

McCall, Robert T., 230, 279
233 East 48 Street
New York City

McConnell, Gerald, 206
330 East 46 Street
New York City

McKee, Terence, 201
343 Lexington Avenue
New York City

McLean, Wilson, 257, 261, 266,
335, 357
314 West 100 Street
New York City

McMullan, James, 287, 296
Push Pin Studios
114 East 31 Street
New York City

McVicker, Charles, 147, 221
230 East 44 Street
New York City

Melia, Paul, 314
3030 Regent Street
Dayton, Ohio

Michal, Marie, 151
35 West 92 Street
New York City

Mikolaycak, Charles, 346
c/o Elizabeth Armstrong
132 East 19 Street
New York City

Modica, Joseph, 104, 299
67 Pendleton Place
Staten Island, N. Y.

252

Utterback, Bill, 23
1907 South Wolf Road
Hillside, Ill.

Valla, Victor R., 130, 222
c/o McKeown Studios
211 East 51 Street
New York City

Veno, Joseph, 210, 320
246 Commonwealth Avenue
Boston, Mass.

Virgona, Hank, 436
41 Unon Square
New York City

VonSchmidt, Eric, 323
532 Black Road
Sarasota, Fla.

Vucksonovich, William, 174
Whitaker Guernsey Studio
250 East Illinois
Chicago, Ill.

Walther, Wolfgang, 111, 399
Bachlettenstr. 47
CH-4000, Basle
SWITZERLAND

Weaver, Robert, 179, 303, 372, 431
337 West 12 Street
New York City

Weller, Don, 28, 184, 232, 316,
367, 422
340 Mavis Drive
Los Angeles, Calif.

Wetli, Hugo, 213
c/o Fortune
Time-Life Building
New York City

White, Charles III, 348, 355
132 East 26 Street
New York City

White, Jack, 332
9337 North Crawford
Evanston, Ill.

Whitesides, Kim, 271

Wilkinson, Chuck, 95
Art Group
1200 Penobscott Building
Detroit, Mich.

Williams, Paul, 96, 123, 430
c/o Frank Lavaty
45 East 51 Street
New York City

Wolin, Ron, 69, 241
711 North Westmount Dr.
Los Angeles, Calif.

Wood, Leona, 114
10567 National Boulevard
Los Angeles, Calif.

Wyeth, James, 67
Chadds Ford, Pa.

ART DIRECTORS

Allner, Walter, 5, 25, 213, 215, 311, 436
Andrews, Fred, 205
Anish, Jack, 357
Antupit, Samuel, 119, 135, 143, 219, 256, 281, 348, 386, 389, 421
Avon, Connie, 420

Baeder, John, 238
Bartlett, R. C., 302
Belsky, Murray, 73
Benkendorf, Bert, 375
Bennett, Archie, 53
Bennion, Stewart, 117
Berg, John, 98, 131, 178, 337, 338, 406
Bernard, Walter, 239
Bernbom, Lene, 42
Bierhorst, Jane, 313
Blanchard, Bob, 350
Bleiweiss, Herb, 13, 95, 97, 108, 161, 229
Blend, Robert, 373
Boege, Ulrich, 49, 280, 441
Boss, Dave, 232, 241, 422
Brewer, Bill, 10
Buckow, George, 140, 249
Butler, Lowell, 14, 159

Cadge, William, 166, 212, 393
Carmichael, Jack, 258
Carr, Allen, 54, 174, 391
Catalano, Al, 206
Cheney, Bob, 33
Chestnutt, David, 186
Chwast, Seymour, 138
Clemente, Tom, 433
Chereskin, Ron, 234
Colby, Gery, 115, 383
Colton, Robert, 269
Core, Roger, 267
Corman, Thomas, 435
Cowman, Irving, 36, 160
Crump, Frank, 183, 404
Danbrot, Bruce, 13, 95, 97, 108, 161, 229

D'Anna, Russ, 145, 152, 255, 403
D'Anna, Russell, 92
Davis, James, 443

Deardoff, Kenneth, 129, 429
Defrin, Robert, 120, 168, 343
Delessert, Etienne, 254, 278, 290, 308
DeLucia, Carlo, 167
Del Vecchio, Pasquale, 171, 319, 394, 417
de Santis, Mike, 262
Dizinno, Hugo, 252

English, Desmond, 74
Epstein, Henry, 43
Evans, Harold, 70
Everhart, William, 416

Fenton, Joan, 51, 76, 154, 328, 434
Fiorello, Phil, 139
Firebaugh, Ron, 285
Fisher, Milton, 207
Flaherty, Jim, 208
Forbes, Bart, 84
Forgione, Robert, 128
Foster, Bill, 354
Fromm, Paul, 407

Gabor, Harvey, 315
Gangel, Richard, 6, 27, 121, 303, 309, 409
Gauna, Frank, 369
Gillum, Vern, 355
Glaser, Milton, 239, 253, 291, 372
Glassman, Bob, 325
Glixon, David, 1, 172, 381
Gold, Bill, 312
Gotfryd, Alex, 442
Graham, John, 136, 177, 387, 408
Gregory, Bill, 376
Grossman, Alvin, 132, 322

Haber, Zelda, 60
Hagen, Dorothy, 149, 153, 182
Halfant, Jules, 321
Hallock, Robert, 88, 260, 330
Hammond, Gordon, 431
Harvey, Bill, 32, 57, 78, 364, 426
Harvey, William, 80, 374
Hatfield, Lynn, 31, 272, 290
Hauser, Jaques, 111
Hedin, Donald, 9, 52, 114, 209, 223, 247, 405

Heicklen, Alan, 133
Herdegan, Richard, 90, 236
Herr, Margo, 50, 202, 217, 347, 362
Hess, Richard, 81, 141, 339
Hill, Marg, 310
Hine, Ken, 9, 52, 114, 209, 223, 247, 405
Hinrichs, Kit, 11, 41
Holland, Brad, 87, 189
Holman, Bob, 295
Hopkins, William, 137
Hurlburt, Allen, 67, 157, 176, 246

Immerman, Sol, 425

Johnson, Dan, 314

Kalfayan, Onnig, 144
Kalish, Lionel, 116, 286
Kappes, Werner, 171, 214, 271, 428
Kartebei, Bruce, 293
Kearney, Hal, 21, 64, 68, 71, 83, 94, 204, 332
Kent, Norman, 164
Kerchoff, Morris, 2, 7, 20, 346, 359
Kipp, Glenn, 221
Kleeger, Burt, 230, 279
Klemin, Diane, 268, 432
Kner, Andrew, 414, 427
Kolomatsky, Eugene, 30, 327, 384
Kramer, Carveth, 257

Lardis, Jack, 187
Larkin, Denis, 266
Lavengood, James, 101
Lawton, Robert, 379
Lee, Jeannette, 99, 283, 307
Leone, Leonard, 118, 142, 306, 323, 336, 392
Lessin, Andrew, 77, 86, 89
Linkhorn, Forbes, 147
Lubalin, Herb, 250, 324, 326, 423
Lynas, Gerald, 382
Lynch, Paul, 284
Lyons, Rick, 110

Maharry, Robert, 222
Mainieri, Louis, 366
Mallett, Windsor, 72, 431

Marshall, Gary, 184
Marunas, Carol, 190
Massie, Reg, 93, 191
McBane, Emmet, 48
McDonald, Robert, 224, 412
McKenna, William, 17
McKinney, Charles, 18
McLaine, Tom, 47, 233
McLean, Wilson, 261
Medvecky, Zoltan, 331
Menell, Don, 335
Menken, Howard, 139
Mentkin, Bob, 243
Meyer, Dietmar, 16
Miller, Murray, 44, 360
Monath, Norman, 201
Munce, Howard, 165
Munowitz, Kenneth, 15, 415

Nobel, Louise, 398
November, David, 418

Osaki, George, 103, 146, 150, 378

Parker, Judi, 34
Parker, Phil, 298, 377
Paturzo, George, 109, 390
Paul, Arthur, 8, 23, 63, 107, 124, 179, 248, 296, 300, 365, 424
Pearson, Robert, 40
Persky, Mort, 163
Peter, Harald, 58, 62, 112, 244, 396
Pizzi, Elmer, 218, 397
Poggenpohl, Andrew, 45, 162, 345, 439
Portuesi, Louis, 188, 237
Powell, Dean, 349

Quint, Bernard, 125

Ramsay, Bob, 175
Reed, Jack, 410
Reed, Walt, 235
Risom, Ole, 216
Robson, Jack, 231, 276
Rosenberg, Sid, 388
Rosenthal, Eli, 156
Rubenstein, Mort, 418
Ruffins, Reynold, 24

Russell, Edward, 3
Russell, Tony, 11, 41

Salisbury, Mike, 367
Sanchez, Rudy, 267
Sanford, Henry, 200
Schmid, Eleonore, 308, 333, 370
Schoenfeld, Norman, 169
Schulman, Phil, 127
Schwartzman, Alan, 287
Scott, Hilda, 26, 113
Scudalari, Bob, 270
Seltzer, Abe, 139
Seltzer, Isadore, 122
Shakery, Neil, 304

Shinn, Gary, 12
Siano, Gerry, 288, 363
Smith, Don, 231, 276
Smith, Ernie, 19, 56
Smokler, Jerry, 227, 265
Sneider, Kenneth, 44, 173, 360
Snider, Suzanne, 332
Sorel, Edward, 22
Staub, Charlotte, 183
Stead, David, 411
Steir, Pat, 273
Stermer, Dugald, 59
Stevens, Martin, 55, 242
Storch, Otto, 214, 226, 271, 344, 394, 417, 428
Stuart, Kenneth, 170, 351

Stubis, Tal, 282

Taback, Simms, 24
Taney, Joseph, 134
Tehon, Atha, 250
Tinkelman, Murray, 352

Underwood, Muriel, 371

Van Demark, Vance, 340
Veno, Joseph, 210, 320
Volpe, Charles, 38

Wachter, Richard, 66
Walker, Frank, 297
Walther, Wolfgang, 399

Wanek, John, 282
Ward, Kay, 173
Weare, Nancy, 277
Weller, Don, 316
White, Bernard, 341
White, Stanley, 361
Wilkinson, Kirk, 79
Wilson, Bradley L., 82

Yablanca, Hy, 65
Yanez, Maurice, 356
Yocum, Dick, 185

Zelcer, Alfred, 263
Zlotnick, Bernie, 46
Zwiebel, Alan, 294

CLIENTS

ABC Television, 43
Air Express, 269
American Airlines, 165
American Export Isbrandtsen Lines, 356
American Telephone & Telegraph Co., 127, 206
Ames Co., / Division of Miles Lab, 266, 304
Armstrong Cork Co., 81
Art Directors Club of Los Angeles, 316
Artists Associates, 334, 352
Artists Guild of N. Y. C., 349
Assumptionists, The, 287
Astra Pharmaceutical Products. Inc., 243
Avril Rayon, 90, 236

Baldwin Piano & Organ, 314
BBDO, Inc., 156
Boodles Gin, 298, 377
Buzza-Cardozo, 10
California Institute Technology, 375
Capital Records, 103, 146, 150, 378
C.B.S., 418
Celanese Corp., 144
Champion Papers, 3
Chase Manhattan Bank, 11, 41
Chemical New York, 331
CIBA, 66, 395
Cincinnati Milling Machine Co., 252
Columbia Records, 98, 131, 178, 337, 338, 406
Curtiss-Wright Corp., The, 411

Dear Love Corp., 234
DeBeers Diamonds, 288, 363
Detroit Red Wings, 115, 383
Dresser Magcobar, 340

Eastern Airlines, 36, 160, 224, 412
Eaton Laboratories, 139
Elektra Records, 32, 78, 426

Famous Artists School, 235
Famous Faces, 138

Garrette Corp., Inc., The, 117
General Cigar Co., 373
General Electric Co., 82, 354
Glenn Printing Co., 105
Goodrich, B. F., Co., 47, 233

Hallmark Cards, Inc., 58, 62, 99, 110, 112, 244, 283, 307, 396
Honda, 228

Kahn, Harvey, Assoc., 122
Key Note Promotions, Inc., 141
Kohler & Sons Printing, 366

Leach Corp., 65
Lincoln Mercury, 185
Local One—Amalgamated Lithographers of America, 88, 260
Lockheed Aircraft, 355
Lubalin, Herb, Inc., 19, 56
Lutheran Church of America, 361

Manufacturers Hanover Trust Co., 294
Manufacturers Mutual Fire Insurance Co., 205
Member Newspapers, 433
M.G.M., 230, 279, 357

National Football League Properties, 232, 241, 422
National Park Service, 416
N.B.C., 30, 136, 177, 327, 384, 387, 408
Neiman-Marcus, 285
New Jersey Bell Telephone, 221
New York Life Insurance Co., 17
Nonesuch Records, 57, 364, 374
Norsworthy Mercer, 379

Pan American Airlines, 200
Pfizer Pharmaceutical 48
Pine State Foods, Inc., 18

Pioneer Moss, 46
Pioneer Systems, Inc., 325

R.C.A. Records, 120
R.C.A. Victor, 168, 343
Revlon, Inc. 55, 242
Reynolds Tobacco Co., 128
Richardson's Extermination, 186
Ruffins / Taback, Inc., 24

Sanders Printing Co., 116, 286
Schering Corp., 267
Scott Paper Co., 231, 276
Seattle Art Directors Society, 12
Smith, Kline & French, 175
Sorel, Edward, 22
Southfield Life Insurance, 410

Tenneco Chemical, 320
Theatre Three, 295
Toronto Life, 284
Trans World Airlines, 208
Travelers Insurance Co., 407
Turn About Records, 190

UNICEF, 317
UNICEF Greeting Cards, 254
United Airlines, Inc., 40, 101
United Artists Records, 369
United Engineers, 218, 397
U.S. Air Force, 61, 100
U.S. Chamber of Commerce, 210
United States Lines, 187

Vanguard Records, 321
Volkswagen of America, 207

Warner Bros. / Seven Arts, Inc., 282, 312
Warren, S. D., Co., 72
Washington Square Press, 425
WMCA, 238
World Art Group, 38

PUBLISHERS AND PUBLICATIONS

AGENCIES

ADVERTISERS

ARTISTS ASSOCIATES

ART STAFF INC.

BAINBRIDGE'S SONS, CHARLES T.

FABER-CASTELL-HIGGINS, A. W.

FAMOUS ARTISTS ANNUAL (HASTINGS HOUSE, PUBLISHERS)

FAMOUS ARTISTS SCHOOL

GRAPHIS ANNUAL (HASTINGS HOUSE, PUBLISHERS)

GRUMBACHER, M., INC.

KIMBERLY-CLARK CORPORATION

LAVATY, FRANK, & JEFF LAVATY, ASSOCIATE

MANDEL CO., ESTELLE

NEELEY-MULVEY ASSOCIATES

PHOTOGRAPHIC COLOR SPECIALISTS, INC.

PLAYBOY MAGAZINE

READER'S DIGEST

SEVENTEEN MAGAZINE

SPORTS ILLUSTRATED

THOMPSON COMPANY, J. WALTER

TIME INC.

WINSOR & NEWTON INC.

PRODUCTION CREDITS

The text in this book is: Helvetica Light
Composition by: Richard Wood Typographers and William Patrick Co., Inc.
Offset plates and printing by: Connecticut Printers, Inc.
Advertisements section by: Bodley Printers, Inc.
The paper is: Black and White Offset Enamel Dull
Paper supplier: Andrews/Nelson/Whitehead Publishing Papers
Binding cloth by: G. S. B. Fabrics Corp.
Bound by: A. Horowitz & Son
Jacket and endpapers printed by: Middlebrook Press
Production supervision: Irma Lavaroni, Hastings House
Assistant to the publisher: James Moore, Hastings House

As this book is printed in process colors, we regret that the original colors
of some of the illustrations reproduced here have been altered.

ILLUSTRATORS

ADVERTISEMENTS

Jane Sneyd, Advertising Director

ARTIST: BILL HOFMANN

THE SOULS OF BLACK FOLK
BY W.E.B. DU BOIS

ARTISTS:
DONN ALBRIGHT ● RICH-
ARD AMUNDSEN ● JOHN
ASARO ● ISA BARNETT
● BARBARA BERNAL ●
HARRY BORGMAN ● RO-
BERTA CARTER CLARK
● MAC CONNER ● GIL
COHEN ● GERRY CON-
TRERAS ● LOU CUNETTE
● KEN DAVIES ● RIC DEL
ROSSI ● BERNARD D'AN-
DREA ● TOM EATON ●
MAE GERHARD ● ETHEL
GOLD ● JOE GORNALL ●
PAUL GRANGER ● RICH-
ARD GREEN ● CATHERINE
HANLEY ● JOHN HANNA
● ERASMO HERNANDEZ
● BILL HOFMANN ●
RUSS HOOVER ● GORDON
JOHNSON ● SALLY
KAICHER ● RONNIE
LESSER ● STANLEY MELT-
ZOFF ● MARIE MICHAL ●
RAUL MINA MORA ● DEL
NICHOLS ● TAYLOR
OUGHTON ● JAN PALMER
● JOSEPH PHELAN ●
DON PULVER ● LINDA
SMITH ● PHIL SMITH ●
GEORGE SOLONEVICH ●
ALTON S. TOBEY ● KYUZO
TSUGAMI ● MICHAEL
TURNER ● THOMAS UP-
SHUR ● PATRICIA VILLE-
MAIN ● CECILE WEBSTER
● RON WING

REPRESENTATIVES: BILL NEELEY ● RANDY MULVEY ● CHARLES GARDNER

Neeley-Mulvey Associates Inc. **Art & Photography** 45 West 45 Street, New York CI 6-3660

Discover the now artists in the pages of Sports Illustrated

Portrait from The J. Walter Thompson Art Collection

J. Walter Thompson Company, then...

and now.

PLAYBOY®
REQUESTS THE
PLEASURES OF YOUR
PORTFOLIO

ART PAUL
ART DIRECTOR
PLAYBOY MAGAZINE
THE PLAYBOY BUILDING
919 NORTH MICHIGAN AVENUE
CHICAGO, ILLINOIS 60611

artists

NORMAN ADAMS / RICHARD AMSEL / GEORGE GIUSTI / BOB HANDVILLE / KEN NISSON
NORMAN LALIBERTE / FRED OTNES / GENE SZAFRAN / MURRAY TINKELMAN
REPRESENTED BY BILL ERLACHER / JIM GYSEL / KIRSTEN HANSEN
ARTISTS ASSOCIATES / 211 E. 51 ST. / NEW YORK, N.Y. 10022 / PL 5-1365-6

WHAT DO THESE DISTINGUISHED
ARTISTS, ILLUSTRATORS AND DESIGNERS HAVE IN COMMON?

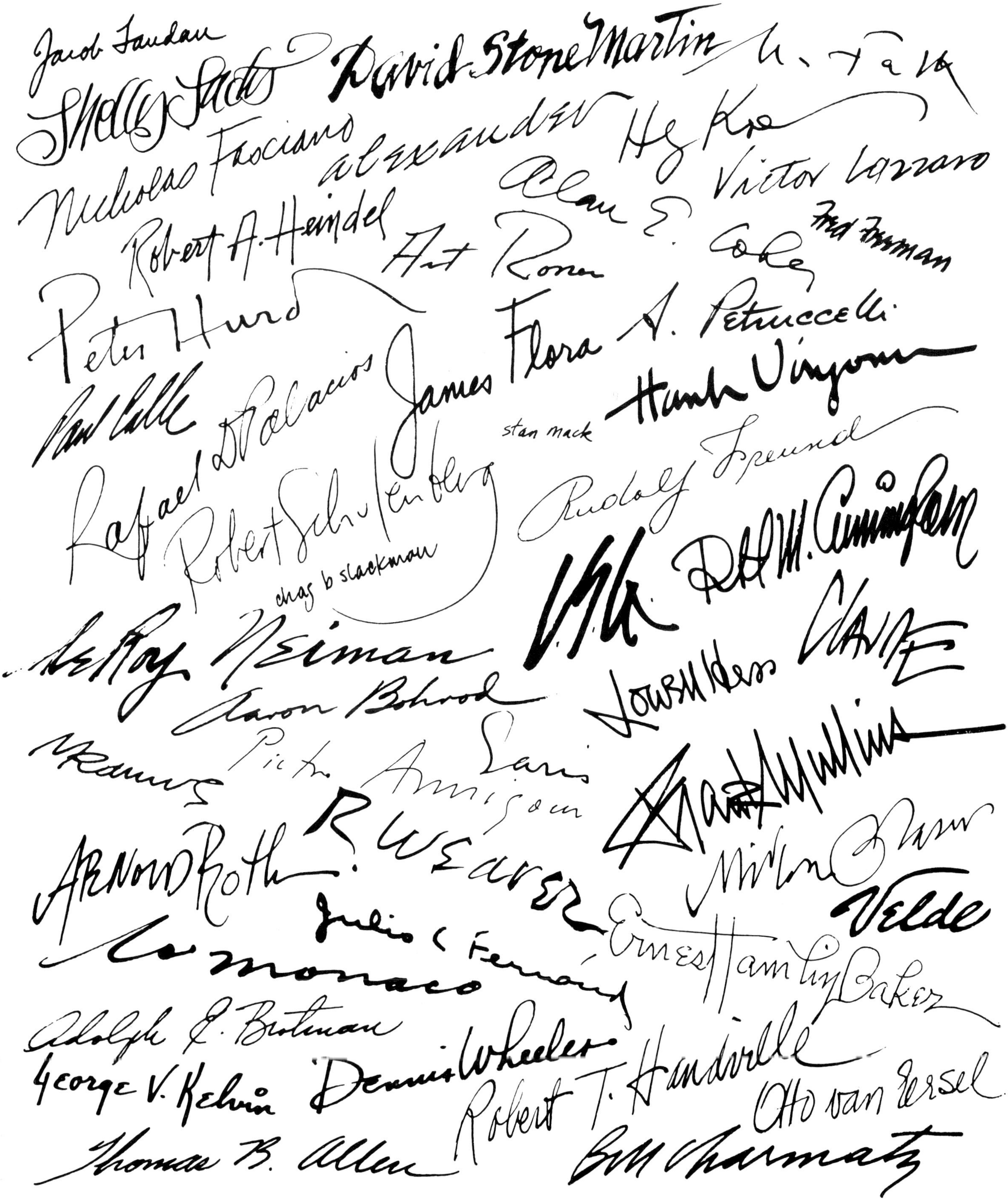

[page of handwritten signatures]

Jacob Landau

Shelly Sacks

Nicholas Fasciano

David Stone Martin

alexander

Hy Roe

Victor Lazzaro

Robert A. Heindel

Art Rosen

Alan E. Cober

Fred Freeman

Peter Hurd

Paul Calle

Rafael D. Palacios

James Flora

A. Petruccelli

Hank Virgona

Robert Schulenberg

stan mack

chas b slackman

Rudolf Freund

RM Cunningham

LeRoy Neiman

John Kess

CLARKE

Aaron Bohrod

Pietro Annigoni

Hara

Mark Mullins

Arnold Roth

R. Weaver

Mirko Ross

Velde

Monaco

Julio Fernand

Ernest Hamlin Baker

Adolph E. Brotman

George V. Kelvin

Dennis Wheeler

Robert T. Handville

Otto van Eersel

Thomas B. Allen

Bill Charmatz

TIME INCORPORATED

ARE YOU INTIMIDATED BY ITS SIZE?

Reader's Digest
reaches the largest audience around.
People have faith in The Digest.
Can you create a Digest ad that will attract, excite,
motivate its 41 million adult readers?
Others have.
Reader's Digest has faith in you.

FAMOUS ARTISTS SCHOOL HAS PROBABLY DEVELOPED MORE MONEY MAKING/PRIZE WINNING ARTISTS THAN ANY OTHER ART SCHOOL IN THE WORLD.

Like Carl Kock of Chicago, Illinois who works for an art studio and has already won 5 gold medals. He's exhibited with the Art Directors Club of Chicago, the Society of Typographical Artists, the Society of Illustrators. And does work for clients like: Playboy Magazine, General Motors, Upjohn Co.

Or Robert Heindel who can boast a Time Magazine cover on his list of achievements.

Or Mel Kane who has made it as a full-time television commercial film producer in California.

Or a painter like Edith Ferullo, whose agent, Las Olas Gallery in Florida, sells her paintings to known collectors at prices of $500 and more.

Or Douglas Chaffee of Apalachin, New York, who won the bronze medallion at the National Association of Industrial Artists annual contest. And has a series of ten Gemini illustrations on permanent display at the Smithsonian Institute in Washington, D.C.

If you know anyone who would like more information about our training, just tell them our address is:

Famous Artists School,
Studio A-6362, Westport, Conn. 06880

Frank Lavaty & Jeff Lavaty, Associate. Artists' Representatives
Complete portfolios available. 45 East 51st St., New York, N.Y. 10022
Phone ELdorado 5-0910

ART

John Gilbert

Lemuel Line

John Berkey

Allan Mardon

Birney Lettick

Gervasio Gallardo

Paul Calle

Paul Williams

These artists are represented exclusively by **Frank Lavaty Associates.** Also represented are George deLara, Lou Feck, James Flora, Pete Hawley, Gene Jarvis, Paul Lehr, Lou McCance, James Mitchell, Bernard Perlin, Ken Riley and Earl Thollander.

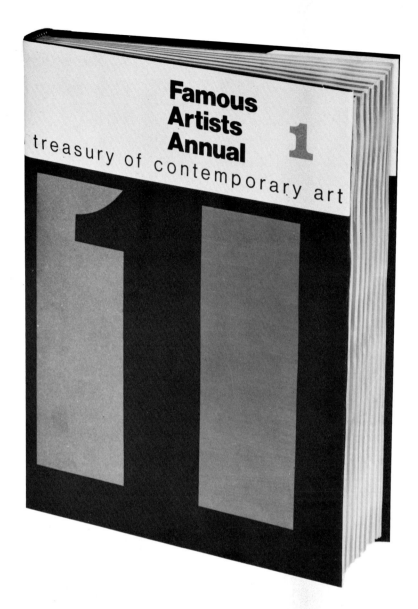

Famous Artists Annual 1

A TREASURY OF CONTEMPORARY ART

Here is what is going on in the world of art today. Covers painting, graphics and sculpture as well as commercial art from advertising and magazine illustration to children's books, posters, record album covers and art for theatre and films — a treasury of styles, techniques, mediums, composition, design and use of color *by the top professionals in all fields.* Examples by the most exciting and influential artists of our time: Briget Reilly, Milton Glaser, Andrew Wyeth, Peter Max, Tomi Ungerer and Leo Lionni. There are pages of magazine and advertising art by such outstanding artists as Austin Briggs, Norman Rockwell and George Giusti. And pages of paintings, graphics and sculpture by Shahn, Albers, Stella, Rauschenberg, Dali, Picasso, Calder, Marisol, Moore and others. For every reader and particularly for students of art and illustration, it should be a revelation of possibilities and a permanent source of inspiration and ideas. Published in collaboration with the Famous Artists Schools, Inc.

248 pages, 9⅝″ x 12⅜″, 251 black-and-white illustrations in monochrome gravure, 110 illustrations in four-color gravure.   **$25.00**

VISUAL COMMUNICATION BOOKS

Hastings House, Publishers, Inc.   10 East 40th Street • New York, N. Y. 10016

PUBLICATION: SEPTEMBER 1970
THE NEW 1970/1971
graphis annual

INTERNATIONAL ADVERTISING GRAPHICS   Edited by Walter Herdeg

At your fingertips for instant
reference, bristling with ideas
and inspirations is this record
of the year's outstanding work
in posters, advertisements, booklets,
magazine covers, trademarks
and in film & television.
Get *one* idea and the book will
have paid for itself.
This 19th annual has 250 pages,
928 Illustrations, 72 pages in color,
text in three languages, plus
detailed index, all printed on
coated stock, bound in sturdy
Buckram linen, with handsome
dust-jacket. How can you do without
it? You can't. The price: only $19.50.

VISUAL COMMUNICATION BOOKS

Hastings House, Publishers, Inc.
10 East 40th Street • New York, N. Y. 10016

THE EQUALIZERS

Strike out, armed with only a crossbow, on the trail of a rather pugnacious bear. Or try harpooning a shark in the surf. The hunt is on as modern man tries to outwit his quarry armed only with crossbow, harpoon, bola, falcon or boomerang. They're THE EQUALIZ-ERS in our latest promotion, as we take an insider's look at the ancient weapons man chooses to even the odds. Come along as we head afield on Kimberly Opaque . . . a medium weight paper that's equal to the challenge of many heavyweights.

To get your set of posters on brilliant Kimberly Opaque . . . just ask your Kimberly-Clark Sulphite Business Papers distributor for THE EQUALIZERS. Your set will come to you rolled in a tube . . . ready to frame or decorate the walls of den or office.

✳ Kimberly·Clark

BUSINESS PAPERS
Neenah, Wisconsin 54956

KIM 497K   This is Kimberly Opaque, White, Vellum Finish, Sub. 80, printed in 4 colors with PMS Process Inks.

There are **85** beautiful, brilliant, smooth-flowing, opaque Winsor & Newton's DESIGNERS' superfine GOUACHE water colors — the finest you can possibly buy

Designers, (who love them) don't waste a drop!

In addition to the range of 85 colors, priced from 60¢ per No. 5 tube, Designers' Colors are also available in the following sets:

Introductory Set of 10 No. 5 tubes **$6.00**

SET NO. D1: *Aluminum box, hammertone grey finish, Size 4¼″ x 10⅛″, fitted with 12 No. 5 tubes of Designers' Superfine Gouache Colors and 3 sable brushes* **$13.50**

SET NO. D2: *Deluxe metal box, size 8¼″ x 3⅞″, with grey hammered finish complete with sliding palette, Fitted with 10 No. 5 tubes Designers' Superfine Gouache Colors and 3 brushes* **$16.50**

SET NO. D11: *Heavyweight black enamelled box, size 4½″ x 9½″, fitted with 11 No. 5 tubes of Designers' Superfine Gouache Colors, 3 sable brushes and sliding palette* **$15.00**

Winsor & Newton Inc.

555 Winsor Drive, Secaucus, N. J. 07094

Canadian Agents: The Hughes Owens Co., Ltd., Montreal
Californian Dist.: The Schwabacher-Frey Co., San Francisco

HE HAD LITTLE CHOICE...

When the Stone Age artist wanted to express himself esthetically, he had a limited choice of surfaces — the wall of his cave or perhaps the bark of a tree.

To say we've come a long way would be an understatement. Today's artist has thousands of surfaces he can work on. However, when you consider Illustration Board surfaces, you need consider *only three:*

BAINBRIDGE

#169 ROUGH ▪ #172 SMOOTH ▪ #80 MEDIUM

Approved for Kromo-Lite, Fluorographic and DropDot processes.
This trio of quality boards will meet <u>all</u> your needs!

At art supply stores everywhere!

- ▪ ILLUSTRATION BOARDS
- ▪ MOUNTING BOARDS
- ▪ BRISTOL BOARDS
- ▪ SHOW CARD BOARDS
- ▪ FABRIC BOARDS
- ▪ KEETON KUTTER

CHARLES T. BAINBRIDGE'S SONS / Famous for quality since 1869
20 Cumberland Street, Brooklyn, N.Y. 11205

A
ALCORN, John
ALEXANDER, Martha
ALLEN, Laura Jean
ALLEN, Tom
ALTOON, John
ANTONAKOS, Stephen
AVERSA, Piero

B
BALET, Jan
BARDEN, Anne Marie
BARKLEY, James
BECK, Jack Wolfgang
BENNET, John M.
BERG, Joan
BISHOP, Isabel
BLACKWELL, Garie
BLANCH, Arnold
BLANCHARD, Carol
BOUCHÉ, Louis
BOZZO, Frank
BROOK, Alexander
BROWN, Donna
BROWNING, Colleen
BRYSON, Bernarda
BURRIS, Burmah

C
CAMERA, Sheila
CARLE, Eric
CARPENTER, Mia
CATO, Bob
CHARMATZ, Bill
CIKOVSKY, Nicolai
COBER, Alan
CONDAK, Cliff
COOPER, Jim
CORCOS, Lucille

D
DALY, Tom
D'ANDREA, Bernard
DAVIS, Gladys Rockmore
DAVIS, Paul
DILLON, Leo
DOBKIN, Alexander
DUBOIS, William Pène

E
EVERGOOD, Philip

F
FASALINO, Teresa
FOX, Lorraine
FRASCONI, Antonio
FREDENTHAL, David

G
GALLARDO, Gervasio
GILL, Bob
GILLEN, Denver
GIOVANAPOULOS, Paul
GLASER, Milton
GLUCKMANN, Gregory
GRAY, Susan
GWATHMEY, Robert
GIULIANI, Vin
GUNDELFINGER, John

H
HAMPTON, Blake
HANE, Roger
HAYES, Marvin
HAYS, Phil
HIRSCH, Joseph

J
JOHNSON, Doug
JOHNSON, Guy
JONSON, Jim

K
KANE, Irene
KAPLAN, Alan
KARASZ, Ilona
KARBAN, Barbara
KARLIN, Eugene
KARP, Leon
KAUFMAN, Joe
KLIROS, Thea
KUNIYOSHI, Yasuo

L
LAMBERT, Saul
LANDAU, Jacob
LAURENCE, Jacob
LEE, Doris
LEVERING, Robert
LEVI, Julian
LEWITT, Sol
LINDNER, Richard

M
MAFFIA, Daniel
MARSH, Reginald
MARTIN, David Stone
MARTIN, Fletcher
MARVIN, Frederic
McDANIEL, James
McMULLAN, James
MOCNIAK, George
MORGAN, Jacqui
MORFOGEN, Elaine
MORROW, Tom

N
NESS, Evaline
NIVOLA, Constantino

O
OLSON, Maribeth

P
PALLADINO, Tony
PARKER, Robert Andrew
PEAKE, Bob
PERL, Susan
PONTBRIAND, Roger
PRESTOPINO, Gregorio

R
REFREGIER, Anton
ROMBOLA, John
ROSE, William
ROSELLI, Luciana
ROSENFELD, Richard
RUDDOCK, Martha

S
SCHNEEBERG, Robert
SELTZER, Isadore
SHAHN, Ben
SHIELDS, Bill
SHIMIN, Symeon
SHORE, Robert
SIPORIN, Mitchell
SLOAN, John
SOYER, Isaac
SOYER, Moses
SOYER, Raphael
SPANFELLER, James J.
STONE, Gilbert
SULLIVAN, Robert
SUZUKI, Mary
SWEAT, Lynn

T
TAM, Ruben
THOMPSON, Mozelle
TINKLEMAN, Murray

V
VINCENT, Tom
VIRGONA, Hank

W
WARHOL, Andy
WEAVER, Robert
WHITESIDES, Kim

Z
ZAID, Barry
ZERBE, Carl

Where does a girl go for a good art education? **To** *seventeen*

For the past twenty-five years

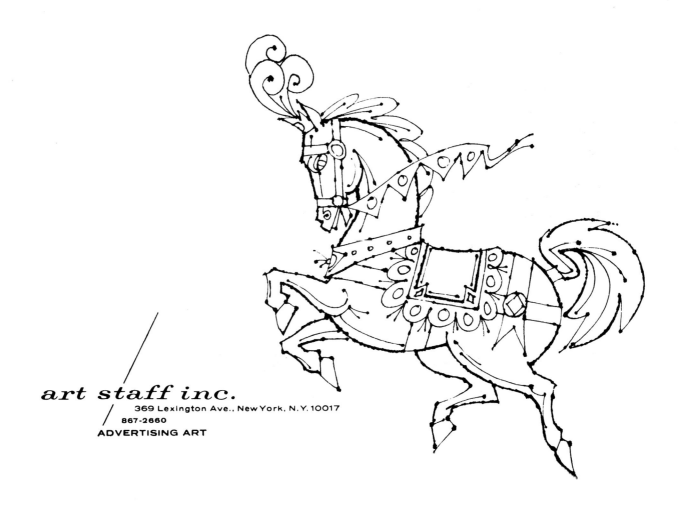

art staff inc.
369 Lexington Ave., New York, N.Y. 10017
867-2660
ADVERTISING ART

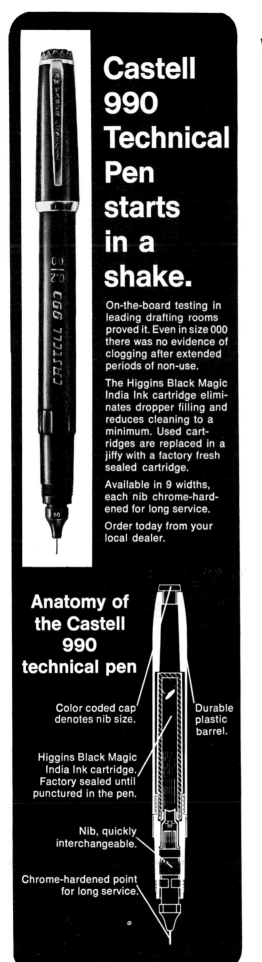

Why do I use Hyplar® colors?

Because Grumbacher makes it, and I trust their
acrylic colors. There are other reasons, too: I can
save a lot of time, because Hyplar is fast drying, and
use any technique I wish—Oil Color, Water Color,
Tempera, and Glazing. I get a wide color variety
in a hurry from the 32 brilliant, intermixable Hyplar
colors in 2 oz. tubes, (white & black in larger tubes)
and in jars from 2 oz. to 32 oz.
You can quote me..."The designer and illustrator
should not be without Hyplar." M. Grumbacher Inc.
460 W. 34th St., New York, N. Y. 10001